RING OUT!

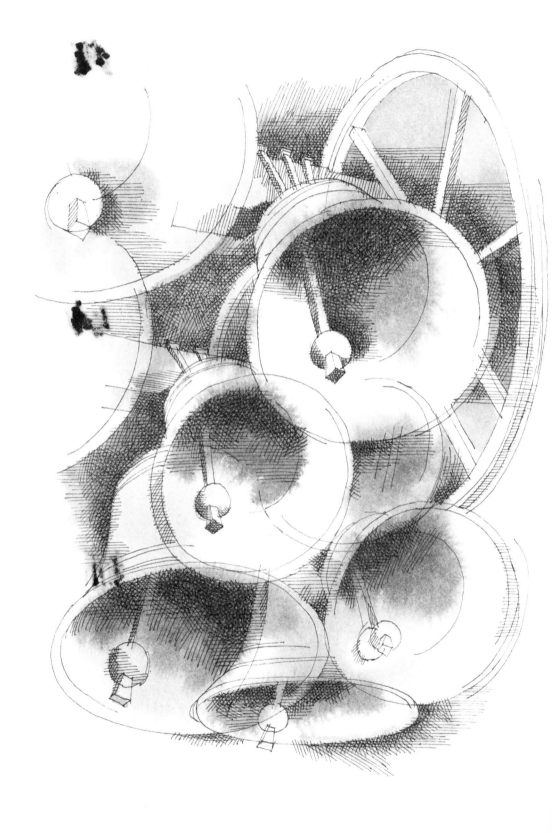

 RING OUT!

A BOOK OF BELLS

by Jane Yolen

Drawings by Richard Cuffari

A CLARION BOOK
The Seabury Press
New York

Library of Congress Cataloging in Publication Data
Yolen, Jane H
  Ring out! A book of bells.
  SUMMARY: Presents the development and uses of bells and their effect on man's life over the centuries through a combination of folk tales and facts.
  Bibliography.
  1. Bells—Juvenile literature. [1. Bells]
I. Cuffari, Richard, 1925–   illus. II. Title.
CC207.Y64   789'.5   74-4043
ISBN 0-8164-3127-2

To the craftspeople we know and love:
  Jon and Bobbin, leatherworkers
  Michael, Jim, and Meg, potters
  Rosanna and Jacki, silversmiths
  Pat, weaver
who have helped open us to the beauty
of handwork and the making of crafts

A NOTE OF THANKS

I want to thank the many friends who sought and found bell material for me or in other ways helped with the production of this book: Sid Fleischman, Dot Leone, Sue Alexander, Pat Wood, Peg Cantwell of the Hatfield Library, Shulamith Oppenheim, Dale Cope, Nancy Frazier, Rosalind Clark, David Stemple, and Alma L. Harward, a founding member of the North American Guild, and ringer at Smith College and Church of the Advent, Boston.

Contents

Introduction

What is a bell? An easy definition would be that a bell is anything which produces a ringing tone when struck. That could include hollowed wood, a piece of flat metal, some kinds of gourds, and the shaped metal with a clapper or tongue we know so well. It is the tone that is important.

Indeed the word "bell" comes from the old Anglo-Saxon word *bellan*, "to bellow." Of course, other countries have other names. *Campana* and *campaña* in Italy and Spain, *cloche* in France, *Glocke* and *klokke* in Germany and Scandinavia, and *clog* in the Gaelic countries. In Chinese, the name for a bell is onomatopoetic—it sounds like what it is: *tsiang-tsiang*.

The sound of the bell is the sound of the world's past. Ancient Chinese and Peruvian civilizations kept pace with the day by the sounds of the bells. The people of medieval towns and monasteries rose, ate, prayed, and retired to the sound of a constant ringing, jingling, jangling, and pealing of bells. Men at work on the sea, women teaching in country schools, children waiting impatiently for Christmas morn, all counted on bells in the past.

But bells are part of the world's present too. Bicycle bells still warn pedestrians off roads. Electric alarm bells wake late sleepers. Chimes announce a caller at the front door. Electronic bells call out classroom changes. And clocks still ring the hours and the New Year in all over the world.

The bells in our present are very vocal in recalling our past. I was especially reminded of this last year as I stood in a crowded ringing room at Smith College in Northampton, where I had gone to school, where I have taught, and only a few miles from where I live. Six college girls, one college boy, and the Dean of Smith College stood at the ropes. At a signal, they began to haul on the bell ropes, ringing the changes on their eight bells. Their clothes were different from ringers in the past: blue jeans and sweaters instead of coats and vests and trousers of the all-male ringers of days long gone. But they rang as lustily and as happily and with as much dedication as those of generations past.

And overhead, not caring whether they were ringing in 1973 or 1873 or 1073 for that matter, the great bronze voices called out: bam-bam-bam, bo-bo-bo, over and over and over again.

JANE YOLEN

Phoenix Farm
Hatfield, Massachusetts

To call the fold to church in time,
    We chime.
When joy and mirth are on the wing,
    We ring.
When we lament a departed soul,
    We toll.

                    —*old rhyme*

Chapter 1

The Ancient History of Bells

It is said that, long ago, when the Chinese sage Confucius sat dining with his students, they talked of the many marvels on the earth.

One of the boys remarked, "I have heard stones sing."

The others laughed at him. "Long Chan hears everything sing," said one. "His big ears are continually ringing."

But the sage quieted them. "All things have voices, though we do not always hear them. Why not stones?" He turned to the tall, skinny boy the others called Long Chan. "Tell me of these singing stones."

"O Master," said Long Chan, "they are not ordinary stones sitting by the river bank or on the mossy forest floor. They are large stone bells of graduated size. Each one is hung from a large wooden frame. I have seen a man play upon the *Pien Ching*, as it is called. He hits each stone in turn with a stick. And they sing, Master. The stones, how they sing."

"Singing stones," said Confucius thoughtfully. "I would like to hear this marvel."

Long Chan smiled a great smile. "I think I can find the man and bring him here to play upon his stones."

"Do so," commanded the sage. "To hear a stone's voice would be a marvelous thing."

A few days later, Long Chan ushered a man into the sage's room. "This is the man I spoke of," he said. "The one who plays upon the *Pien Ching.*"

The students helped the man set up the wooden frame and the stones. One by one, from the smallest to the largest, the sixteen stones were hung upon the frame.

The man bowed to Confucius and then took a stick from his sleeve. He turned to the frame and began to hammer upon the hanging stone bells. Each gave out a ringing, the big stones deep sonorous tones, the smaller stones high sweet tones. The man played one, then another tune.

All the while the students sat on the floor and listened. Confucius, sitting on a thin silken cushion, listened too.

When the man had finished and turned to bow once more, the students clapped their hands and shouted. But Confucius was still.

It is said that he remained that way, quiet and unmoving, for three months. And for three months not a morsel of food passed his lips, though his students, fearing for his life, tried to feed him.

On the first day of the fourth month, the sage spoke. "I have heard beauty," he said. "I have heard dumb stones sing. Surely I shall never hear anything sweeter."

Not everyone has been so moved by the sound of bells that he has given up eating. But certainly bells have had the power to move men throughout their long history. The voice of the bell has sung, summoned, wept, warned, scolded, and mourned. And the men, women, and children listening have been moved.

Because bells speak the fundamental language of music, they speak all languages. And because they speak all languages, they have been almost universally known from their beginnings. Mentions of bells have been found in the writings of the ancient Chinese, in Assyrian palaces, in Etruscan tombs, and in the ruins of the Mayan and Mixtecan civilizations. Yet like gunpowder, printing, porcelain, and kites, bells were brought to a peak of development in the Orient long before they became well known in the West.

Inscription on a bell in Anvers, 1658: "There is neither speech nor language but their voices are heard among them."

Where men and their civilizations flourished, bells flourished, their voices touching all fields of human endeavor. Bells have tolled for men and women and children, individually and collectively, at their births, at weddings, and at deaths; in times of peace and in times of war. They have rung in historical events, opened markets, located lost animals, warned ships in danger, called together the worshipers and scholars, amused musicians, aided magicians, and frightened away devils and imps.

Bells have even taken on quasi-human qualities. There are tales of bells that refuse to sing if insulted, bells that sweat blood when frightened, and bells that cry tears. There are stories of bells that have taken revenge on those who tried to injure them, and even one Japanese bell that was said to have shrunk from the touch of a vain woman.

For over four thousand years, the history of man and the history of bells have been linked.

The first bells were no more than simple gourds or nutshells struck with a piece of wood. Then clay models were made. Finally the metal bell was

Natives in Africa struck upon hollowed wood bells. The Chinese had wooden temple bells called chung.

discovered, probably accidentally by one of the first workers in metal. However the true art of bell-making did not begin until men learned to make bronze, the oldest of the alloys, by mixing copper and tin. The making of metal bells can be traced all the way back to 3000 B.C., the Bronze Age.

One of the first types of bronze bells was the small crotal used by herdsmen. Tied around the necks of animals, these tiny jingly bells helped the herdsmen find missing cows and sheep. Over 36 centuries old, this bell has not changed its basic shape in all those years. The crotal is a little sphere with small connected holes in the side. It has a tiny ball within. The ball was first made of clay, then metal. Christmas bells and sleigh bells are crotals.

Crotals were also mentioned in the Bible as adorning Aaron's robe. Any slight movement caused the crotals to jingle and tinkle, a warning according to scholars that a mortal was approaching the holy sanctum of God. Crotal bells have been so popular that, of all the ancient bells discovered in tombs and buried cities and other archeological digs, more crotals have been found than any other kind of bell.

"Upon the hem pomegranates of blue and purple and scarlet . . . and bells of gold between them round about."
—Exodus 27.

Bells go back a long time. Three thousand years ago in Peking, a massive bell was struck by the city watchman four times a night, its loud deep voice calling out the hours. Almost 30 centuries ago, the Mayans were making thousands of tiny exquisite gold bells. In Egypt 2,500 years ago, many religious feasts were announced by the ringing of bells. When the Egyptian tombs were first opened, the archeologists discovered many small bronze bells within, bells used for horses and oxen and sheep, and bells with which servants woke their masters.

The costumes of ancient Persian kings and Hebrew women, virgins, and boys were decorated with small bells during the days of the Old Testament. Around the time of Christ's birth, the Romans announced the time of public bathing and public business with the insistent clamoring of small hand bells. The Jewish author Josephus, who lived from A.D. 37–100, reported that the golden roof of Solomon's temple had bells upon the top to chase away birds.

But the tale about bells that puts their invention farthest back in time is one told by the Oriental author Dionysius Bar Salibi. He ascribed the invention of bells to Noah. Bar Salibi insisted that Noah had created bells in order to summon his workmen to the ark three times a day.

When the palace at Nineveh was excavated, a copper cauldron was unearthed containing 80 small round bells, a treasure some 2,000 years old.

Chapter 2

The Middle History of Bells

In the Middle Ages, the Jutes of Jutland were at war with the Swedes. Peter Gyldenstierne, the Jute leader, led an army of men into one small Swedish farming village after another. Finally, they rested their march in a large town. Two bells in the town tower, unmindful of the Jutes' victory, were calling out the hours in their silvery voices.

"I must have those bells," said Peter Gyldenstierne. "They must come back to Jutland with me."

But neither he nor any of his men could think of a way to take the two bells from the tower without doing injury to the tower and the bells.

Gyldenstierne rounded up the peasants of the village. He made them all stand in a circle before the church. "Tell me how to take the bells from the tower," he shouted at them, "or you shall all die."

The peasants stood mute. They would not give away the secret of their beloved bells. But finally one man spoke out. "Promise me you shall provide for my wife and children and I will show you how to get the bells."

"Done," said Peter Gyldenstierne.

The peasant showed the Jutes how to collect sand from the shore and pile it high on two sides of the tower. Then the peasant climbed the tower, cut the chains that held the bells, and let the two of them roll gently down the hills of sand.

Once the bells were safely out of the tower, Peter Gyldenstierne pointed at the peasant. "Seize him."

"But sire, you promised . . ." the peasant cried out.

"I will keep my promise," came the reply. "Peter Gyldenstierne *always* keeps his promise. I will provide for your wife and children. But you—you are a traitor to your town. You shall take the place of the bells."

Peter Gyldenstierne had the peasant hanged in the church tower for all to see.

Why was Gyldenstierne so harsh to the peasant? And why were the bells so important?

In the Middle Ages the bells of a town were thought to be its soul. Every free town from the thirteenth century on owned its own set of bells. If ever a town were captured or taken by a superior power, the first step in conquest was for the conqueror to take away the town bells. That was symbolic; it showed that the city's liberties were also being taken away.

Bells grew in importance in Europe the way Christianity grew in importance. Their growths were closely linked.

The first Christians, on pain of death, had had to hide their faith. They met in the dark of night, in underground caverns and caves. As long as the Christians had to hide, there was little bell ringing in Europe except for the hand bells that announced the baths or opened the markets, or the tiny jingly bells on the bridles of war horses and the herds of cows and sheep.

When their faith became legal and Christians began to build churches, worshipers were at first summoned by messengers who banged together large wooden clappers known as sacred boards. The sound was dull and clacking and joyless.

Then in A.D. 400 in Campania, Italy, the bishop of Nola whose name was Paulinus had a strange idea. He thought that striking a large brass kettle would make a "joyful noise unto the Lord," just as it said in the Bible. So he ordered that a kettle be hung above the church and had it struck loudly and resolutely with a hammer when it was time for the people to assemble. Paulinus' invention was certainly louder than the sacred boards, its tones happier than the clacking call of the clappers. But whether the congregation thought it a truly joyous noise will never be known. Nonetheless, the kettle-bell remained. Ever since, according to legend, large bells have been called in Latin *campanoe* after the town and smaller bells *noloe* after the bishop.

The Feast of St. Paulinus is celebrated every July 25th in small Italian towns. Youngsters buy clay bells for a penny and ring them gaily all day.

Supposedly Bishop Paulinus' kettle was the first of the large church bells, the giants that hang above houses of worship and cry out in loud demanding voices. However, it would be another hundred years before there would be founders and foundries able to cast the giant bells for all the churches that desired them.

Meanwhile, smaller hand bells for calling together the worshipful became popular. Missionaries carried hand bells to all corners of the globe. The hand bells announced the missionaries' coming and assembled their flocks. Often these bells

The Bell of St. Patrick's Will can still be seen in the Museum of Ireland. It was the one the saint was said to have carried himself.

were crudely made four-sided bells. Such quadrangular bells were cut from sheet iron, the plates bent in two and fastened together with iron rivets. The entire bell was then coated with bronze.

These small crude bells were especially popular with the Irish missionaries. When St. Patrick came to Ireland from Gaul (now France) in 440, he brought with him bishops and monk-craftsmen (metal smiths and braziers among them). It was said that whenever Patrick founded a monastery, he set a bishop over it and the smiths to making monastery bells.

By the middle of the sixth century, the first foundries, run by monks, were casting bells several tons in weight. These European foundries were only seven hundred years behind the Chinese. Somehow the sophisticated method of bell casting had never traveled west of Asia where bronze bells had been made as far back as 220 B.C. Such casting had to be reinvented by itinerant founders who cast bells in each European courtyard where a bell was to hang.

Big bells became so popular that, by the beginning of the seventh century, they were commonly used in the Italian churches. Pope Sabinaus is often credited with encouraging their usage in 604. The Italians were so pleased with their big bells they started sending out the giant bronze monsters with their missionaries. It made traveling slow and more difficult but, according to one old account, the bell's voice inspired the heathens.

Egbert, Archbishop of York, wrote "Excerptions" in 750. It ordered all priests to ring bells at the proper hours.

It was only a short time after that, in the eighth century, that Turketul, the abbot of Croyland Abbey in England, hung the first peal, or set of tuned bells. And the Croyland peal's bells were named as musically as they sounded: Pega, Bega,

Tatwin, Tusketyl, Betelin, Bartholomew, and Guthlac. If one bell could summon the worshipers from nine miles round, what a sound a set of tuned bells could make. A glorious calling, singing, ringing, even up to the gates of heaven itself.

By the 900's, bell towers were being raised all over Europe. Edward the Elder ordered walls and towers erected across the island of England. His son, Athelstan, passed a most peculiar law in 926. Any Saxon churl or peasant could become a thane or nobleman if he possessed three things: 500 acres of land, a church on his property, and a bell tower beside his church.

From that time on England has been known as "The Ringing Island."

And so bells became a most important part of church life. Since church life and everyday life were totally linked in the Middle Ages, the sound of bell ringing was as common as the sound of a laugh.

Kings often gave a bell or a peal of bells to a church or monastery. A monarch who wished to honor a town that had pleased him might give it a ring of bells. Conversely, if a town had done a ̄ing some wrong, it was often deprived of its bells as a punishment.

Furthermore, whoever owned the town's bell or commanded it controlled the town. It was the bell ringer who assembled the town guard, announced danger, or called together the people of a town. It was the bell ringer who could overpower even the most moving speaker with the loud weighty tones of the bell. This is why for many years bell ringing was considered a political activity, and the ownership of the bell one of the conditions for making a peasant noble.

Bell ringing was so political, in fact, that in 1453, when the Turks captured Constantinople, an edict was passed forbidding the ringing of bells. Sultan Mahomet Bey, the conqueror, declared that Christians could "have their churches and burying places. Only *let them not ring bells*." Sultan Bey used as his excuse that Arabs and Turks believed that the ringing of bells disturbed the repose of departed souls. But behind that religious reason was a much more important political notion: he who controlled the loud voice of the bells controlled the communications and the heart of a city.

By the middle of the Middle Ages then, bells were everywhere in Europe. Their voices were as varied as the human voice, and more insistent. They functioned as newspapers, announcing births, deaths, victories, and defeats. They called the people to rise in the mornings, to open their shops, to come to market, or put their bread in the lord of the manor's ovens. They sounded the alarum when fire threatened. They were the call to prayer and the call to sleep.

Each event was rung on the bells with a different voice. The alarum was sounded by the bells calling lowest to highest. When the bells all began leaping and thundering together, the citizens knew to run out for a meeting in the streets.

Bells also rang in some of the greatest single tragedies known to man. In 1282, the ringing of the Sicilian Vespers on Easter was the signal to slaughter 8,000 French men, women, and children who were living on the island of Sicily. On August 24, 1471, the midnight bells ringing in Paris tolled the start of the St. Bartholomew's Day Massacre in which 10,000 French Protestants, called Huguenots, were killed.

Just as the citizens knew the power of the bells, so did their rulers. In the 1500's, an English edict went out that "wherever any bells were rung to raise rebellion only one bell is to be left in the steeple in memory thereof." Even harsher was the punishment inflicted upon the bells of Carlisle Cathedral which had rung out in joyous tumult

when Bonnie Prince Charlie, the pretender to the
English throne, entered the city. The bells of
Carlisle were silenced by law for 180 years there-
after by the angry and unforgiving English kings.

Chapter 3

Bells and the Religious Life

Brother John lay sleeping. On his hard pallet he dreamed that all the angels in heaven were ringing the morning bells. "Ding-dong, ding-dong," they cried at him, their high voices insisting: "Time to arise."

Brother John sat up suddenly. It was no dream. The *signum* was squalling, ringing away. All the monks at the abbey knew that when the *signum* was rung, it was time to awaken.

Brother John arose from his pallet, but only as far as his knees. He said his morning prayers quickly on the cold stone floor. Then he arose more fully and went to the wash basin. He poured cold water over his hands from the pitcher and dabbed at his face. Already the *squilla*, the bell for breakfast, was calling shrilly. As usual Brother John was late.

Brother John's entire day was bounded by bells. All the monks in the abbey were used to the silence in their lives that was broken by only two things: prayers and bells.

When the abbot wanted to issue a special order,

the *codon* was rung. Brother John, who tended to straggle, was one of the monks warned by the harsh call of another bell, the *petasius*. And more than once for his tardiness Brother John had been called to a scourging for disobedience by the shrilling of the *corriguincula*, the "little correctress."

For Brother Peter, who sang in the choir, there was the *nola* that helped cue him in. For Brothers Jeremiah and Stephen, who sometimes napped through evening prayers after a long day tending the garden, the *noctula* and *dupla* were a special nuisance, for they roused them from even the soundest sleep.

But those were not the only bells in the monks' lives. They all recognized the large bells that tolled the time for prayers. Six o'clock: prime. Nine A.M.: tierce. Twelve noon: sext. Three P.M.: nones. Six P.M.: vespers. Nine P.M.: compline. And matins and lauds were rung in the early hours between midnight and prime.

It was the voice of the monastery bells that controlled the lives of all who dwelled within the walls, from the shrill hand bells that called for corrections to the insistent jingling of the Sanctus bell at the mass to the deep, mournful tolling that told of a monk's death. Because the bells could be heard wherever a monk might be working or praying, eating or sleeping, waking or dying; and because the different kinds and sizes of bells could be made to say different things, the bell was the single most important voice to the brethren of a medieval monastery. It was, to them, the voice of God.

But bells in religion are far older than Christianity. Indeed, bells have been, from earliest times, associated with both magic and religion, with fakery and faith. "The magic metal" is an old name for the bell.

Early religions used bells for calling together the worshipers and for calling the gods themselves. Gongs were hung before Oriental temples and rung as a signal for all to gather. The Roman emperor Augustus ordered bells hung before the temple of Jupiter to summon suppliants. The lamas of Tibet rang hand bells to announce themselves ready to pray. The Jewish scrolls of the law, the *torah*, wore bell-decorated finials that sang out when the prayers were opened to be read. Mayan gods were summoned to sacrifices by bells that were hung on the feet and wrists of victims. Egyptian priestesses rang *sistrum*, metal hoops with attached bells to call the goddess Isis to come and hear their prayers.

Aztec gods, Tezcatlipoca, Tlaloc, and Huitzilopochtlii were represented as carrying bells.

There were even some cultures in which bells were, themselves, the gods. In the hill tribes of Southern India, the cowbell was thought of as a god. Each sacred herd of buffalo had a bell buffalo, or leader cow. When the bell buffalo died, ·her eldest daughter inherited the rank and bell. The sacred bell was worn by the bell buffalo for three days and three nights in order to consecrate it. Then the bell was removed and never worn again in the lifetime of that particular cow. Instead the bell was lodged in a priest's house where only the priests might look upon or touch it.

Christian Ireland also has a form of bell veneration, for the missionary bells are preserved with great care by special families.

However, the most consistent theme in the religious use of bells has been the power that bells are supposed to have over the evil spirits who plague humanity.

In most of the ancient religions it was believed that a loud noise could drive away demons.

Whether drums drumming, horns howling, or bells ringing lustily, loud sounds "would drive away the persecuting demons a greater distance." When Christianity supplanted earlier pagan faiths, the priests and people still clung to that belief.

One of the earlier tales about St. Patrick tells how the saint was facing a large horde of devils from the North with no weapon in his hands save a small quadrangular bell. St. Patrick rang the bell with all his might, yet he could not defeat the powerful enemies. With a last desperate effort, he flung the bell into their midst. The clanging bell so frightened the devils and imps then that they raced away screaming loudly, but no louder than the din of the bell. And the evil spirits did not come back to Ireland for seven years, seven months, and seven days. The bell St. Patrick tossed, battered from its adventure, is known as the "Broken Bell of Brigid" and can still be seen in Ireland today.

One nonbeliever was Bishop Lattimore who wrote in 1552: "If the holy bells would serve against the devil . . . no doubt we would soon banish him out of all England."

Belief in the power of bells to drive away devils lasted many years. There are still some vestiges of it in church thinking today. The ritual of excommunication with a ringing bell, a Bible, and the snuffing out of a candle still exists in some conservative ceremonies. And there are those who still believe that a baby born on the chime hours—3, 6, 9, and especially midnight—have second sight and can cast out devils.

"Cold iron" was believed to be useful against witches and goblins by the Norsemen.

From the fifth century on, though, just ringing bells loud enough to frighten devils was not the only way to keep evil away. The church fathers began to put two and three and even more bells together as a necessary part of the ritual of the Christian church. Bells were rung before, during, and after services as a constant reminder of God. A poor parish would no doubt use the same bell for many uses—angelus, matins, and all. But a richer parish would take pride in having separate bells with distinct voices for every task.

And, since the secular life was so closely linked to the religious life in the Middle Ages, a farmer's life was as regulated by the church bells as a monk's.

Farmer James lay sleeping. On his straw bed, he dreamed that all the angels in heaven were ringing the morning bells. "Ding-dong, ding-dong," they cried at him, their high voices insisting: "Time to rise."

Farmer James sat up suddenly. It was no dream. A bell was ringing, its pattern unmistakable. Three strokes, pause, three strokes, pause, three strokes, pause, nine strokes. It was the angelus bell. He must get up. If the angelus was ringing, it was six o'clock and time to rise. His wife slipped out of bed by his side. They kneeled together on the packed dirt floor and began their prayers.

Today was no ordinary day. It was a Sunday in March of 1550, the day of rest. A day of baptism. Yet Farmer James knew he did not have time to rest, especially if he was to go to the baptism. The animals had to be fed first, and then he and his goodwife Joan would go to church.

At church Farmer James would hear more bells yet. First the great slow tolling would call the farmers and villagers from as far away as nine miles round to come and gather and pray. Then the pardon bell would ring, before the service, and again after, reminding them all to pray that their sins be pardoned.

During the service itself, the priest's acolyte would ring the high-pitched little sanctus bell as

The Angelus was also called Ave or Gabriel bell. It was introduced by Pope Urbanus II in 1095.

the priest raised the host, the wafer, and said in
Latin: "Sanctus, sanctus, sanctus," which meant
"Holy, holy, holy." The bell, also known as saunce,
sacring, or holy bell, was so shrill and insistent that
even if Farmer James had fallen asleep during the
long service, it would awaken him for that most
important part of the Mass.

When a sermon was to be preached in church,
a special sermon bell was tolled. At Farmer James's
church, the sermon bell was inscribed: "I ring to
sermon with a lusty bome, that all may come and
none stay at home." Its deep weighty tones signaled that a deep weighty sermon would be
preached that day. Farmer James was glad of the
sermon bell, for on the days that it tolled he was
usually able to find an excuse to stay at home.
Sermons were always long and full of threats of
eternal hell-fire and Farmer James did not like
them.

The Puritans of the late 16th century were more interested in the sermon than the service and would stay away from church if the sermon bell did not ring.

If Farmer James and his goodwife Joan missed
the early service because a cow was calving or the
goat was sick, they could still get to church in time
for the last service. When the compline rang out,
they knew it was time for the last religious service
of the day.

But this particular Sunday, Farmer James and
his goodwife did not wait for the sermonless service or for the last service of the day. Today was
special. It was the baptism day for the newest
church bell in the tower. The local lord and his
lady were coming all the way from Lancaster to
stand as godparents for the bell. All the villagers
and farmers within the sound of the bells would
turn out for the christening. And so it was. Farmer
James and his goodwife Joan and their neighbors
and friends watched the priest anoint the big bell,

sing psalms over it, and bless it with holy water. Then the bell was named; Peter it was called, after the blessed saint.

"'Tis good it is blessed," said Joan to Farmer James. He agreed. Now the bell would have special powers. It would help put out fires, abate the wild storms, and protect all of them from pestilence. And thinking these good thoughts, Farmer James and Joan followed their neighbors to the church hall where a magnificent feast had been spread. Truly, baptising a bell, Farmer James thought, is a blessed thing.

Farmer James would not soon forget the baptism. He remembered it each holy day when the bells rang out in joyous tumult together—Christmas and Easter and on the New Year.

Farmer James was not an educated man. But had he heard of the strange book that a priest, Frater Drabicus, was to write in 1618 he would doubtless have approved. The good father penned a 425-page tract that proved his contention that the principal employment of the blessed in heaven would be the continual ringing of bells. For Farmer James and Brother John and all the common folk of the Middle Ages such a thing was not hard to believe. After all, bells were so much a part of their lives on earth, it was quite probable that bells would be an important part of their lives in the hereafter.

Baptizing a bell can be traced to the days of Charlemagne, in the 780's.

"Arise and go about your business."—bell from St. Ives, England, 17th century.

Chapter 4

Town Bells

In the fourteenth century, there lived a young lad who was apprenticed to a merchant and the lad's name was Dick. Dick Whittington.

Young Dick had nothing in the world but a cat. And since he lived on the top of the merchant's great house in a garret under the eaves, where the rats ran about at night and troubled his sleep, a cat was more than a pet. It was a helpful friend.

One day the merchant Fitzwarren was preparing a ship to send to the far shores of Barbary. He told each member of his household that they might send a single item with the ship to try their luck in foreign trade.

Poor Dick had nothing but his cat. So with great sighs and fond farewells, he sent the cat away. However, once the ship and Fitzwarren had sailed off, Dick found himself alone with no friend at all in the great house. He was mocked and beaten upon by the other servants. So Dick decided to run away.

With nothing but the clothes upon his back and a pair of well-worn shoes upon his feet, young Dick

set off. He walked as far as Halloway and there he
sat down upon a stone to rest his weary legs. From
the distance the bells of the church Mary le Bow
called out a tune. They seemed to be singing to the
tired lad:

> Turn again Whittington, Lord Mayor of London.
> Turn again Whittington, Lord Mayor of London.

Dick could scarcely believe his ears, but turn
again he did. He fairly flew all the way back to
Fitzwarren's house.

When he got there, Captain Fitzwarren was
home from the Barbary shores, his coffers filled
with gold. And most of the gold belonged to Dick.
For the kingdom of Barbary had been overrun by
rats. The king had purchased Dick's own cat for
an enormous sum.

Dick Whittington became a rich man. He mar-
ried Fitzwarren's pretty daughter and, true to the
song of the bells, he became Lord Mayor of London three times. But he never forgot his cat.

The story of Dick Whittington has been told
again and again for hundreds of years. And many
people believe it to be true. But it is only true in
part. There was a London mayor Richard Whittington who was mayor three times. And there is
a church Mary le Bow whose famous Bow Bells
are known throughout the world. People who were
born in a certain part of London call themselves
Cockneys and proudly say that they were "born
within the sound of the Bow Bells." But the real
Richard Whittington was not a poor serving lad
who became rich because of his cat. He was born
the son of a merchant and grew up in a wealthy
family.

However, the tale of Dick Whittington, his cat, and the bells is now a popular legend. And many a poor man living in a city might wish such fortune on himself. For through the ages city folk have listened to the ringing, jingling, and tolling of many different bells. In the days before the insistent chatter of television and radio, of electric clocks and alarms that are set off electronically when fire or thieves intrude, the loudest and most compelling voice in a city or town was the voice of the bell.

Town and city bells, also known as common or mote bells, helped regulate the life of a municipality. These bells, according to an old inventory of 1552 "ronge when any casualtyes chaunce and for ye gathering together ye inhabytants. . . ." Often such bells hung in the church tower and were rung not only for religious services but for every conceivable town happening and event.

Nottingham had a common bell in 1315.

Gate bells rang out in most medieval towns as a signal for opening or closing the town gates in the great walls that surrounded the community.

The common bell rang to open the market. Legally in the Middle Ages a market could not even begin until the bell had sounded. "It is ordyred that no person opyn ther sack or set ther corn to sale afore the hour of ten of the bell or els the undernone bell be rongyn" read the law in 1478. The undernone was another name for the market bell. There were heavy fines for "forestalling," that is buying or selling before the bell rang.

Plutarch reported bells opened fish markets in first century Greece.

The Bellman and Crier walked the streets of every large city in the Middle Ages calling out the hours as he rang his bell. "Oh yes, oh yes (Oyes)" the Bellman called to announce the latest news, in the days before there were newspapers. He as-

sembled interested listeners with the clanging of
his hand bell.

City vendors had recognizable hand bells too,
bells that matched their street cries. The bells fore-
warned of the vendors' coming. For example, there
was a dustman's bell, a muffin bell, a rag-and-bone
man's bell. Today we have the ice cream trucks
whose bells are as easy to recognize for us as any
of the vendors' bells of long ago.

In 1850, the English passed
a law prohibiting vendors'
bells because of all the noise.

But the two most familiar bells of a city long
ago were the alarum and the curfew.

The alarum, alarm or tocsin, was rung loud and
long to warn of fire, invasion, or revolution. The
sound was a horrifying din, for the alarum was
rung by an unusual method. Either the bell was
struck continuously with an iron rod or, as often
happened, the clapper was grasped by hand and
hammered against the inside of the bell. The ancient tocsin at Antwerp, cast in 1316, was named
"Horrida," and it seems a perfect name for such a
bell.

The ancient fire bell in
Sherborne Abbey is inscribed
"Lord, quench this furious
flame; Arise; run; help; put
out the same."

Related to the alarum was the fire bell for, in
some cities and towns, the alarum was rung only
for the larger disasters. A separate bell or bells or
ringing system existed for the more common oc-
currence of fire. The most common method of ringing for a fire on a peal of bells was to ring them
backwards, that is from lowest to highest. There
is no other bell ringing like it and it is immediately
recognizable. One of the bells in the peal at St.
Ives in England carried this inscription:

When backwards rung we tell of fire.
Think how the world shall thus expire.

And in some towns, a bell code was developed to
explain to listening firemen which part of the city

was ablaze. Our modern fire stations use a similar kind of code with their electric bells.

The curfew bell, according to a famous poem, "tolls the knell of parting day." It has a curious history. In France in the ninth century, when houses were made of wood with thatched roofs, it was very easy for a serious fire to start. All that was needed was a spark from the cooking fire or from the fire that warmed the house. One house would set another on fire and soon an entire small town would be in flames. So a metal cap or fire cover, called a *couvre-feu*, was invented. Each evening when it got quite dark, a bell would be rung in the town's church or meeting hall to remind all the townspeople to use their *couvre-feu*.

When William the Conqueror, a Frenchman, conquered England in 1066, he brought the *couvre-feu* idea with him. The English could not pronounce the word correctly and changed the word to *curfew*. William's curfew was certainly an antifire measure, for English houses like their French counterparts had roofs thatched with straw or rushes. But William's motives were not entirely pure. The curfew was also a very practical way to keep watch on any nightly meetings of dissidents and troublemakers.

Since William's time, the curfew has been abolished or brought back whenever a ruler has felt the need to keep his citizens abed at night. Besides England and France, curfews have rung in practically every country at some point in their history. The Pilgrims brought the custom across the ocean to America.

Marco Polo reported a curfew in Peking where a large bell in a central tower was struck with a heavy wooden mallet each night.

The time of curfew has differed from country to country. Sometimes towns within a country have chosen to ring their curfew at strange hours.

Throughout most of England, for example, the curfew has sounded at eight o'clock. But at Oxford, one of England's most famous university towns, the school's Great Tom rings out curfew at nine o'clock each night with 101 strokes. In Boston, Massachusetts, curfew sounded at nine o'clock until the end of the nineteenth century.

The curfew has been so important to so many places that one of England's towns notes with pride that its evening bell has rung every day for the last eight centuries.

Curfew, alarum, market, or mote, bells have been important to the smooth running of the world's centers of population for hundreds of years. As the Dutch say: "Good schools and good bells are two signs of a well-managed city."

"Our voices shall with joyful sound
Make hills and valleys echo round."
—bell in Ewell, England, 1767.

Chapter 5

Country Bells

The Greek slave Aesop used to tell this tale: All the mice in a certain house crept into the hole of one for a meeting. They had to make a decision. One by one they had been falling into the claws of the mighty cat that lived in the house. Something had to be done.

"And done quickly," said the oldest and wisest mouse. "For if we cannot solve this problem, we shall have to move far away."

The mice nodded their heads and looked sagely at one another but no one had a suggestion.

Suddenly one mouse jumped up. He waved his tiny forefeet in the air. "I have it. I have it," he squeaked. "We shall tie a bell around the neck of the cat. Then we shall always hear him, jingle-jingle, whenever he approaches. In that way, he will not be able to catch us unawares again."

The other mice were delighted. They clapped their forefeet together and spun about upon their tails. And they fell to hugging and kissing and shouting huzzahs.

"Just a minute," shouted out the oldest and

wisest mouse. The others fell silent but with sour looks upon their faces. They did not want to stop their celebration. "Just a minute," the old one called again. "It is all very well, this plan of yours. But tell me this—who amongst us is brave enough to bell the cat?"

And so the mice had to move.

The moral of this story, as Aesop used to point out, was not to make plans that could not be carried through.

Belling cats and other animals is at least as old as the 600's B.C. when Aesop the slave was alive. And it is probably a good deal older than that. Throughout history, a strange variety of animals have worn bells: cows, sheep, goats, dogs, horses, llamas, yaks, ducks, pigs, turkeys, geese, elephants, hawks, reindeer, and coconut-picking monkeys of Malay among them.

The first belled animals were flocks belonging to ancient shepherds. The shepherds belled their sheep so that they might locate the animals should any wander. The shepherds also believed that the sound of the bells made their sheep grow fat. Later only the lead sheep was belled and was known as the bellwether, wether being the word for a neutered sheep.

Today the word bellwether means leader, usually of an unthinking crowd.

The Greeks and Romans also belled their flocks to frighten away predatory animals who might try to attack the sheep. The jingly sounds of the bells were so unnatural that they signaled to any wild animal that there was a man nearby. In fact, bells were so important to the well-being of the Roman flocks that the great emperor Justinian, who lived in the A.D. 500's, passed a law about them. Anyone who stole a bell from a sheep or ox, the law read,

would be whipped as a thief. If the animal were lost because its bell had been taken, the bell thief would have to pay the cost of the animal to the owner.

Cowbells have always been common throughout the world. They can be found on sacred cows in India and on Swiss cows high up in the Alpine pastures. In Switzerland cowbells have had special significance. During the semi-annual trip to the mountain pastures and home again, there is a kind of cow pageant in which each cow wears a bell appropriate to her size and status in the herd. The lead cow's bell may weigh as much as twenty pounds, so heavy in fact that she cannot possibly graze and must be hand-fed by the cowherd.

In India, cowbells have served several purposes. Not only have they been used for locating lost animals, but according to Indian herdsmen, the bells also frighten poisonous snakes. Sometimes in India, bells are fastened between a bullock's horns because it's a convenient place to put them.

All over the world horse bells have been found. Small jingly bells on harnesses and saddles have been discovered from Japan to Peru. Riders with the Mongolian hordes, Roman legionnaires, medieval knights, South American Indians—all have fastened crotals to the trappings of their mounts. Muleteers in the Basque country strapped conical bell towers to their mules. Swiss horses at the annual spring *Sechseläuten* still gallop madly about laden with tuned bells.

From the belling of the Lapland reindeer herds comes the tradition of Santa's jingling sleigh.

In Scandinavia the reindeer herds are belled. Such bells are especially useful in heavy snowstorms when it is difficult to locate an animal by sight. And silent sleighs moving in a blizzard jangle out their warning bells. Similarly, frequent sandstorms in the Mideast forced owners to bell their camels. The constant chattering of the camel bells has kept many a caravan together. Camel bells come in all shapes and sizes. Often they hang on strings, 2–20 bells a string, from a board on the camel's back. The use of camel bells is an ancient tradition. Drawings of them have been found on the walls of the capital of old Persia.

In India, where elephants are work animals, bells are hung about their necks. The animals are turned loose each night to forage and can be located quickly in the dense growth by the sound of the bell. The bells are huge and made of hard wood. Each bell has two wood clappers attached *outside*. The bell cord runs through the clappers and around the elephant's neck. When the animal moves, the clappers clank noisily against the side of the bell.

Besides herdsmen, hunters too have belled animals. Some hunters bell their dogs when hunting in thick cover. When the bell sound stops, the hunter knows his dog has found a bird and is stopped still, pointing.

Bird-baiting, a method of hunting frowned upon by real sportsmen, was often accomplished with a net, a light, and a great bell. According to *Jewel for Gentrie*, published in 1614, the bird-baiters went out at night. The book warned: "If you carry the bell, you must have two companions with nets, one on each side of you; and what with the bell and what with the light, the birds will be so amazed that when you come near them, they will turn up their white bellies; your companions shall then lay their nets quietly upon them, and take them. But you must continue to ring the bell; for if the sound of the bell shall cease, the other birds,

For many years the best goshawk bells were made in Milan, Italy.

if there be any more near at hand, will rise up and fly away."

The legs of hunting hawks were also adorned with bells fastened with rings of leather. According to the *Boke of Saint Albans*, the classic falconing text, it was "particularly recommended that (the bells) should not be too heavy, to impede the flight of the bird, and that they should be of equal weight, sonorous, shrill, and musical."

Another use of animal bells was in horse racing. During the days of the English King Henry VIII, a silver bell valued at 3 shillings 6 pence was given "to him who shall run the best and farthest on horseback." From that custom came the saying that a person who is a winner "bears away the bell."

But perhaps the strangest animal bell of all is the caterpillar bell, an exquisite silver bell decorated with reliefs of caterpillars, butterflies, and other insects. The bell was made by the most famous silversmith of all time, Benvenuto Cellini. During the Renaissance it was used by the popes to curse the caterpillars that annually devoured the Italian crops.

Crop bells have also rung through the centuries in farmlands around the world. There was a seeding bell that called farmers to sow their seed. At harvest times, the church bell rang out morning, noon, and night in the rural districts to remind all that the crops had to be harvested. Itinerant laborers would know by the bells when the farmers needed extra hands. The gleaning bell was also rung at harvest time. It sounded at nine in the morning and again at five in the evening to mark the time when gleaners could, by law, go over the fields and pick up for themselves what the harvesters had left.

The Chinese and Tibetans rang bells for rain; the Tyrolese against hailstorms; and in South America bells were sometimes rung to call the sun. The most common weather ringing, however, was to drive away storms.

The storm bells were directly related to the belief that ringing bells drove away devils. As one old text put it, "It is said that the wicked spirits that be in the region of the air fear much when they hear the bells ringing; and this is the cause why the bells be ringing when it thundereth. . . ." As late as the 1920's in small villages in France this custom was still observed, as the church bells clanged to break up the dark clouds that lay heavy and threatening over the vineyards.

A popular inscription is: "Lightning I shatter, the winds I scatter."

So in the country as well as the cities, one of the most common sounds to be heard for centuries has been the ringing, jingling, jangling, tolling voice of a bell.

"I sound to bid the sick repent
In hope of life when breath is spent."
—bell in Dorset, England, 16th century.

Chapter 6

Bells for Cures and Coffins

The priest and the old woman led the madman through the graveyard. The dark night was frightening him, and he struggled to free himself. Yet at the same time, the man hoped the priest and the old woman would not let him go. To be without any comforting hand would surely be worse, here where the shadows dodged among the dead stones.

The three marched slowly toward St. Fillan's Well, the pool whose icy waters were said to be health-giving. The old woman kept up a steady chatter of comforting words, but the madman refused to be comforted.

At the pool's edge, the woman and the priest forced the man gently to his knees. He did not go easily. Then the priest dipped his hands into the water and washed the man's face and sprinkled his head.

" 'Twould be better if we could get him to bathe himself," said the priest.

The woman nodded, but they both knew it was no use. The madman was too frightened to do anything but struggle.

The three rose then, the madman pulled up by his companions. Then they walked with him back through the churchyard to a stunted tree. There a small bell about one foot high was perched atop a gravestone.

"Hold him while I take the bell," said the priest.

The woman obeyed.

The three moved on through the churchyard into the church itself.

"Have you the ropes, Father?" asked the woman.

"Aye, woman. Would I forget?"

They bound the madman then, hands and feet, and set the bell upon his head like a crown.

"Don't move, you daft creature," said the old woman, "and the good saint will cure you of your madness."

The two left him there in the dark and shut the soft sounds of the night away from him when they slammed the heavy oak door.

"If that canna cure him, nothin' will," said the priest. "It cured poor Crazy Margaret, though she spent half her life thinking she was a sow. By the saints, it will cure your old man."

The ritual of the Scottish bell of St. Fillan's Well is well documented, and many a cure is credited to it. But it is not the only bell that has been thought to be possessed of magic powers to cure the sick.

In certain African tribes such as the Ibo of Nigeria, the witch doctor rang his bell as part of the treatment of a patient. Ecuadorian Indians worshiped idols before whom they rang bells to convince the idols to cure an ailing chief. The bell of St. Odoceus, a fifth-century bishop of Ireland, was credited with miraculous powers. After it lost its

An inscription on an English bell: "I drive away pestilence."

clapper, the bell was inverted by the monks who guarded it and used it as a cup. It was said any water drunk from it could heal the sickest soul. Southern Appalachian mothers believed a child might be cured of stuttering by drinking from a bell. And there was a medieval superstition that a bell rope attached to a woman's belt when she was in labor would ease the pain of childbirth. The Houseling bell, sometimes mentioned in inventories of the Edwardian period in England, was a hand bell carried by the priest as he hurried to the bedside of a sick person. It warned all listeners along the way to pray for the one in need.

One Dr. Hering in 1625 proposed that bells be rung to stop the plague that was sweeping England. Many agreed. But the only bells rung for the plague were those that preceded the dead cart to call the living to bring out bodies of those who had died of the plague.

In the late nineteenth century, when most of the miraculous cures wrought by bells were being discredited by scientific thinkers, doctors still believed that bell ringing could be good for the health. As one wrote in 1876: "In bell ringing, the important muscles of the chest, spinal column, and the arms are brought into powerful, steady, and regular motion." He went on to state that the soothing sounds of the bell and the light, pure air of the belfry were all beneficial to health.

If the miracle cures of the bell did not work, and the patient died, bells were again sounded. This time for the dead. The death knell that tolls slowly and forlornly is still a common sound all over the world.

The history of death bells goes back to ancient Greece. In Athens, at the moment an Athenian citizen died, brass kettles were struck loudly and bells rung lustily. The noise was supposed to frighten away the Furies, the frenzied spirits who were thought to pursue the doers of unavenged crimes. In another region of Greece—Sparta—

whenever a king died, the women of a city would run around the streets striking bells. So, according to Herodotus, the people knew it was time to put on mourning.

But it was in England, centuries later, that the art of ringing the death bell became so ritualized that special bells were cast with such inscriptions as: "Remember Death," "Prepare to Die," and "When you die, Aloud I cry." Death and tolling bells were so connected in the English mind that when Dr. John Donne wrote: "Do not ask for whom the bell tolls, it tolls for thee," no one mistook his meaning.

The death bell was, at first, supposed to be rung while a person lay dying so that the faithful might pray for the repose of his soul. As the soul passed over from life to death, the bell was to be rung. And so it got its other names: "passing bell" and "soul bell."

The death knell was also nicknamed "knocks for the dead."

Sometimes, though, a person recovered after the passing bell had rung for him. More often, the sound frightened the sick one who took a turn for the worse and died. For there was no mistaking the passing bell. It was rung very slowly and evenly, and its voice almost seemed to draw the very breath from a dying person.

When an actual death had occurred, the bell ceased its slow even strokes and rang out the "teller strokes," the strokes that would tell or count off the years of the dead person's life. But first it would signal whether the person was a man or a woman, ringing 3-3-3 for a man, 2-2-2 for a woman. Then the counting would begin, one long-drawn-out stroke per minute. The mournful tolling, each stroke like a deep sigh, often stopped people at their daily tasks and they would count along

The tellers were also called tailors, and so, from the 3-3-3 for a man, came the old saying: "Nine tailors make a man."

with the bell and thus know who in the village had died. "A woman, eighty-seven years old," they might say, "why that must be old Maria, the hosteler's widow." Or, "A man, twenty-four, that's young Tom what was courtin' the miller's daughter and caught chill from the millpond."

Elaborate burial customs began to demand more and more of the church bells. The death bell was rung again at the funeral. There it was also known as the death knell or forthfare. The tones were sounded by hand with a soft wooden mallet called the dead striker. And sometimes, especially in Ireland and Scotland, a man ringing a hand bell called the lych or course bell led the procession to the grave. In some areas at the end of the first month and on the anniversary of a loved one's death, many an Englishman paid for the solemn ringing of the obit bell as a memorial.

In England, when the town's own bell ringer died, the bell was tolled with a piece of wool cloth bound round the clapper to "inspire the mind with melancholy."

Two other bells used in funerals were the winding bell, a high-toned bell rung on the day of the funeral as a wailing counterpoint to the solemn tolling of the death knell; and the bearer's bell, a shrill warning to the bearers of the coffin that it was time for them to assemble for their task.

In pre-revolutionary France, the Bellman of the Dead, dressed in robes with gruesome deathsheads and bones decorating them, went through the streets of Paris ringing a hand bell and calling out: "Awake you that sleep. Rise and pray to God for the dead."

Bells were used in funerals of Pre-Colombian Indians.

But the most feared death bell of all was the one in Exeter, England, known as Doom, for it reputedly tolled at all public executions. As the condemned prisoner was led from prison on his long, slow, inevitable walk to the gibbet, Doom called out in low, grave tones. A similar bell was

rung at St. Sepulchre's in London. There the bellman of the church used to recite the following
rhyme to the condemned prisoners of old Newgate
prison:

> And when St. Sepulchre's bell tomorrow tolls,
> The Lord alone have mercy on your souls.

"I am Roland. When I toll,
it is fire. When I thunder,
it is Victory."—bell in Ghent, Belgium, 14th century.

Chapter 7

Bells for War and Peace

It was August, 1914. The sounds of the guns were coming nearer and nearer. Down below the bell tower, in the city streets, men were racing off to war. They were taking up their guns, kissing their loved ones, and marching out to fight for their beloved Belgium against the German invaders.

From his room in the tower, the bell ringer of Antwerp saw all this. And he did his part too. As the men marched down the streets, he played the national songs of Belgium on the carillon, the set of tuned bells that were the city's pride.

But the men who marched out so proudly were soon slipping back in disarray. The Germans had proved too powerful for their small numbers. And as the Belgian men returned dispirited, high above the city in his tower, the bell ringer of Antwerp played the songs to comfort and encourage them.

Comfort was short-lived. For after the Belgians came the Germans. They entered the city and ransacked it. They burned and they looted. The city's streets were filled with screams and cries. High above the streets, the bell ringer saw all this and continued to play the national songs of Belgium on the carillon. While the enemy took the city, there was still that one brave sound floating defiantly above the noise of the war. The bells sang out boldly, loudly: "Do not fear. All will be well. Praise God. Resist."

When the German command realized the bells rang out for resistance, that the bell ringer of Antwerp was putting heart back into his dispirited people, they ordered him found and shot.

But somehow he escaped, and all of Belgium was encouraged by his escape. He spent the next five years, the war years, in hiding. At last the Germans were defeated and the war was over. Belgium was once again free.

When President Woodrow Wilson came to Antwerp to visit, the bell ringer of the city was again in his tower. He played especially for the visiting American. President Wilson and all of Antwerp listened as the notes of "The Star-Spangled Banner" pealed out on the joyous Belgian bells.

It has been said that the ringing of bells is the one noise that is made solely for the glory of God. It is a pretty statement, but not wholly correct. Bells have rung out for many purposes, and some of them have even rung out for war.

When Clothair besieged the French city of Sens in A.D. 610, the bishop of the city ordered that all the bells of St. Stephen's be rung. The clamor of the bells so frightened the barbarians that they gave up the attack and ran away.

Such tricks with bells had been played before. The Greeks had adorned their war horses with small bells and placed other janglers inside their hollow shields. German officers had attached bells

Inca warriors wore crotals on their belts and even smaller janglers on their legs.

to their garments. In the heat of battle, additional noises can disturb and confuse an opponent. Even the ordinary tinkling of a small crotal can melt an enemy's courage.

Just as some soldiers used bells to turn the enemy's courage to fear, others have used bells to turn their own fear into courage. The Maori warriors in New Zealand used to ring a special war bell known as a *pahu* to strengthen their resolve before battle. In Mexico and America, Indian war dances were accompanied by the jangling of bells.

Plutarch, the Roman historian who lived at the time of Christ, noted an odd use of bells in war. He reported that when the inhabitants of the besieged city of Xanthus tried to escape by swimming through the river, the enemy strung belled nets in the water. Whenever a Xanthusian tried to swim to freedom, he would be caught in the net whose jangling announced his capture to the guards.

Napoleon is said to have been moved to tears in a battle only once, when the evening bells of a nearby town recalled his childhood.

And bells themselves have been used to advantage by the conquerors at battle's end. In 997 when the Moors took over Santiago in Spain, they cut down the bells that hung in the Cathedral of St. James of Compostela. The heavy church bells were then brought all the way to Cordoba, a march of over 400 miles, on the shoulders of the Christian captives. There the bells were turned upside down and suspended by silver chains in the mosque of the Great Mazquita. They were filled with aromatic oils and used as lamps. To the Spanish people of the time, there was no worse desecration the Moors could have performed. It symbolized to the Spaniards how completely they and their Catholic faith were subjugated to the Moslems. The return of the bells became a theme that the Christians

When Charles V subdued Ghent, the mighty Roland was unslung from its tower by the French king.

passed down from generation to generation. Father whispered it to son, mother to daughter, "The bells must be returned." But it was not until 1235, 250 years later when the Moors were pushed out of Cordoba, that the bells were indeed brought back. They were cleaned and reconsecrated and returned to Santiago on the shoulders of Moorish prisoners.

Even as late as the 1940's, bells were used in war. In England, during World War II, bells were rung in London streets to warn of coming air raids.

America's famed Liberty Bell, suitably inscribed: "Proclaim Liberty throughout all the land . . . and to all the inhabitants thereof," rang out jubilantly to declare independence from England on July 8, 1776. Brought over originally from England, the Liberty Bell cracked at its first ringing and was recast by American craftsmen in time to ring out defiantly against the British overlords. The British hoped to capture the Liberty Bell during the war, so powerful a symbol had it become to the Americans. But the Americans spirited the 2,000-pound bell away in a caravan of farm wagons hidden, so legend has it, under a large load of hay. The Liberty Bell came home again in 1778, and in 1781, when the British surrendered at Yorktown and the bells of Philadelphia pealed out, the Liberty Bell was the loudest of them all. (It cracked again exactly 59 years later on July 8, 1835 while tolling the death of Chief Justice John Marshall and has never been rung since. It rests in splendor now in the first floor Tower Room of Independence Hall in Philadelphia, a treasured relic of America's fight for Independence.)

Some bells have been melted down in the midst of war to supply metal for cannon. England's Oliver Cromwell ordered the bells of Cork, Ireland, to be so converted when he took the town.

However, for all the wars that have been fought with and over bells, bells have also rung out for peace. After the victory over Napoleon at Trafalgar, the bells of Chester, England, sang out in joy, a merry galloping peal that ended in one deep toll for the death of Lord Nelson who had died winning the fight for England.

There has probably never been a victory within the history of bells when the great bronze voices have not been summoned to sing out for the peace. The clamor of the bells has reminded the citizens again and again of the peace newly won. Yet even amid this happy noise, there is the reminder of the tolling such bells have performed, death knells for the soldiers who died to achieve the peace.

Such joy and such sorrow are but two of the many voices of the bells.

"I ring at six to let men know
When to and from their work to go."
—bell in Coventry, England, Middle Ages.

Chapter 8

Other Uses of Bells

In China, long before the time of Confucius, there lived an emperor known throughout the land as Yo the Great. He was wise where others had been dull, understanding where others had been obtuse, merciful where others had been cruel, and in all things just.

One of the first things that Yo the Great had done when he had become emperor was to order that a giant bell be hung outside the gates of the palace. He caused a large wooden hammer to be placed by the bell's side.

A sign over the bell read: "If you have been treated unjustly, strike me." Thus a person might plead for justice from the emperor himself. And it was said that the voice of the bell cried out for all, whether great or small.

Soon every town in China had such a bell fastened to the wall above the head of the town ruler, be it governor or prince. To the bell was attached a rope a mile or so in length. The rope was snaked out alongside the main road into town and anyone might ring it without fear as long as his cause was a just one. For when the bell was rung, the ruler—by law—had to send for the petitioner and mete out justice. But woe unto anyone who rang the bell without reason, for then the petitioner himself would be punished.

Yo's bell is a particularly good example of some of the many strange and wonderful uses that bells have been put to throughout their history. They have rung for both religious and lay lives; they have rung in towns and they have sung in the countryside; they have rung for births and weddings and for the dying and the dead; they have cried out in war and joyed out in peace, and for a hundred other causes as well.

Bells have also called out servant to master and master to servant. Bells discovered in Egyptian tombs were servant bells used to wake the sleepy masters of the house. Call bells in the Middle Ages, used to summon the servants, were often ornamental. Every great house in Europe owned such bells.

Figurine bells go back to the 700 B.C.s in Greece where they were used as devotional idols.

The bells ranged from the simple silver bells used by Elizabeth I to figurine bells most prized in the reign of Queen Anne in England's seventeenth century. Some of the figurine bells looked like famous people and the clappers were shaped like feet.

The small handbells used for calling servants eventually developed into the house bell which hung like a church bell and was rung with a heavy cord that ended in a fancy tassel. These were especially popular in the 1800's. Other kinds of call bells include the bell to call a storekeeper in his shop, the bell to summon help at a hotel desk, and even the priest's bell with which a parishoner in need might summon the holy father. Today the most common kind of call bell is the doorbell, many of which were first patented in the days of England's Queen Victoria.

A 19th century catalog listed 108 different types and sizes of call bells.

Another use the bell has had is chiming or calling out the hours. The earliest known clock with a bell chime was recorded by the ancient Roman author Julian in A.D. 180. He mentioned the *clepsydra,* a time-measuring device that was operated by water. When the water, which constantly dripped out of a vessel, reached a certain level, it started a mechanism that activated a bell. So the *clepsydra* was the first known striking clock, but it was certainly not the last.

Some bell clocks merely strike the hours. Others play favorite tunes. The most famous clock tune in the world is "Westminster Chimes," the tune that is played by the bells of the British Houses of Parliament in London every quarter hour. The hours themselves are rung out by Big Ben, the Parliament bell, in a loud, important, and some say off-key voice.

The "Westminster Chimes" tune is based on a theme by Handel and was written in 1793 by a composer named Crotch.

Some bell clocks are more exotic yet. They have mechanical figures that strike the hour. One of the most famous sets of mechanical figures is that atop Strasbourg Cathedral. On the first quarter hour, a little mechanical boy comes out and strikes the first bell with an apple. On the second quarter hour, a youth with a dart hits two bells. A man in arms comes out for the third quarter and with a halbert in his hand strikes three bells. On the fourth quarter an old man with a shepherd's crook strikes four bells. After each of these figures in their turn comes the ominous hooded figure of Death, and at each quarter he tries to carry off the strikers one by one. Each time Death is driven back by another me-

The figures are called "clock jacks," "quarter boys," "quarter jacks," or "Jack o' the clock."

chanical figure representing Christ. When the last
quarter hour is heard, Death strikes the hours with
his bone. This fantastic bell clock was made by two
mathematicians, Dasipodius and Wolkinstenius, in
1571.

Clothing also, from times long past, has been
decorated by tiny bells that jingle and jangle as
the wearer walks. Ancient Persian kings and
queens, Hebrew women at the time of the Old
Testament, all witness the fact that bells were part
of the costumes of our ancestors.

All around the world bells have been used on
clothing. The natives of New Guinea made bells
from shells to dangle from their clothing. In Northern Burma, the Naga women used to wear a short
petticoat trimmed with bells, beads, and shells. On
the west coast of Africa, it was the tradition for
grown girls of the Benin to wear an apron consist-
ing entirely of small brass bells. In parts of Asia,
women wore stilt shoes trimmed with fringes of
bells. Fourteenth century German gentlemen jan-
gled as they walked because of the bells trimming
their jackets. And even in the twentieth century,
bells were a part of the costumes of many teen-
agers in the hip scene.

But it is dancers around the world who most
often have chosen bells to augment their costumes,
for the tinkling of the bells made merry accom-
paniment to their steps. Peruvian Indians dancing
with their pipes and tabors in the street tied small
bells to their legs. The Deer Dancers of Mexico
counted bells as part of their outfits, as did jesters
and tumblers of the medieval courts in Europe.
The Morris dancers in England wore bells at their
knees and ankles as well as bells of unequal size

on their garments. The Morris bells were so central to the dance itself that they were given special names: forebell, second bell, treble, tenor, and double.

Transportation, too, has had its bells. At first the animals who pulled carts and carriages were belled to give warning on crowded roadways. Sleigh bells were especially in demand. Then came Conestoga wagon bells, stagecoach bells, and bicycle bells (which often were sold along with a pamphlet on proper road etiquette).

Even when transportation became mechanized, bells remained important. Railroad bells were used both on trains and at depots, where the bell announced the approaching and departing trains. Train bells continue to this very day, but depot bells, after a time, fell into disrepute. As one train company announced in July, 1880, "the ringing . . . interferes by its noise with the telegraph."

Most important of all transportation bells have been the ships' bells. Even today, the ritual of ships' bells divides the time at sea into four-hour watches, when sailors take turns scanning the horizon and keeping an eye on the running of the ship. Before the coming of public address systems in ships, ships' bells were the way of announcing the change in watches. At every half hour, the bell is struck: once at noon, twice at 12:30, three times at 1 o'clock and so on until 4 when eight bells is struck. Then the bells begin all over again: one at 4:30, etc. The term "eight bells" is the one most commonly associated with sailors, for it is the time at sea when the watch changes.

Lighthouses warning sailors away from rocky

reefs and shores also called out with the loud alarum voice of a bell long before motorized sirens or foghorns were invented. Many a sailor was saved from a wreck by the harsh tolling of the lighthouse bell ringing out over the sound of the breakers. Though now most lighthouses are equipped with electronic signals, the smaller bell buoys carry on the tradition. Dotting the oceans, warning of dangers, these buoys carry bells that ring with every rocking wave and warn the sailors of reefs and sandbars that wait for the unwary voyager.

The list of bells goes on and on. School bells, hand bells with shaped wooden handles, once called late scholars to their books. Now most schools have electric bells that signal the end of classes.

Bell charms from Roman times on were thought to keep children safe from harm. And bells have been popular toys throughout bell history, from whistle bell rattles to complicated bell ringers, wheeled bell toys made of tin or iron.

The pudding bell warned the cooks in the great sixteenth century homes that church services were over and the masters of the houses were returning for dinner.

The Ashanti in Africa used bells as weights to measure gold dust.

Spirit bells in America and Europe seemed to jangle by themselves in answer to questions put to them in magic shows and seances.

The bread-and-cheese bell rang nightly during the Oxford college term in England.

Oath bells were used to discover liars and

thieves in Ireland, Scotland, and Wales, for it was believed no one could swear falsely in their presence.

Travelers in Malay used to carry bells that they could ring if they became lost.

The pancake bell rang at 4 in the morning on Shrove Tuesday in Medieval England to prepare the people for Lent. At that time, as part of the preparation for the holy days ahead, the women of the house collected all the suet, lard, and drippings in the house and made them into pancakes for one last treat before the 40-day period of Lent. It was the only time during the year that apprentices were allowed to eat at the table with their masters. As the old nursery rhyme reminded the English folk:

> But hark I hear the pancake bell
> And fritters make a gallant smell.

And finally there is a practice that has grown up since 1876 at America's Centennial Exposition —the commemorative bell. Bells of copper, glass, and ceramics, bells to look at and collect but not to ring, have been sold or given away at the world's great expositions. They are all inscribed with the date and name of the exposition and are much sought after by bell collectors.

It seems as if all of humanity has been touched at some time by the ringing, calling, tolling, of bells. But the most obvious role that bells can play has not been mentioned—Music.

Chapter 9

Bells and Music

It is a damp and foggy day. The streets of London this cold September in 1870 are filled with the noises of vendors calling out their wares, the horses clip-clopping through the streets.

Suddenly around the far corner a happy cacophony is heard, the jangling music of a dozen hand bells.

Children rush down the street, around the bend. Suddenly they come face to face with a strange apparition. A man, one man alone, playing twelve bells at a time. Upon his head, strapped to a band that ties beneath his chin, are two bells; there are two more in each hand, one upon each knee, and two tied to each foot.

What an incredible sight. And what an incredible sound. One man writes to his friend that the bell ringer played "with great adroitness, and performed a vast variety of tunes."

The children want to dance, but their nurse will not let them. They all go home for tea.

The performer in London playing upon his one-man bell band was dexterous, if somewhat silly.

However, playing "a vast variety of tunes" upon bells is not silly; it is a very serious occupation and one which many people have followed for hundreds of years.

Bells singing out recognizable tunes may have begun as long ago as ancient China with the *Pien Ching* that so captivated Confucius. The *Pien Ching* was made up of sixteen stones, rather like an enormous hanging stone xylophone. When the stones were hammered, they gave off distinct tones. Related to this instrument was the *Pien Chung*, sixteen clapperless bells suspended in a similar frame. *Ching* and *Chung* hung next to one another in temples and were played as echoing instruments.

Bells were also a musical instrument in the days of the Bible's King David, 1000 B.C. A famous musician, King David himself supposedly played upon the lyre, the harp, and the bells.

By the early Middle Ages, hand bells were rung by musicians throughout Europe. These bells, taken over from the monks and missionaries by wandering musicians, became very popular in royal courts. Companies of ringers were formed to play tunes, each ringer handling two bells. A leader would keep the ringers together, and many a merry tune was sounded upon those bells.

Double bells of iron known as Ngonge are staples of West African orchestras.

Today school children can learn to ring White Chapel hand bells, so named after the White Chapel foundry in England where the bells are made.

Yet it was really in the fifteenth century in the Low Countries of Europe that the amusement of playing music on a set of tuned bells rose to a state of art.

The first tunes were played on stationary chimes

that were struck with a hammer. The chimes were tuned to the diatonic scale—that is eight progressive notes that had no half steps between. As far back as 1432 in England, chimes were mentioned. "Richard Roper," one church account reads, "was paid 20d for mending the chymes in Norwich Cathedral."

The word chime comes from the Latin cymbalum or cymbal.

Chimes remained diatonic. Then along came carillons. The first carillons were a set of four hanging bells. But soon the bells grew in size and number, and the name carillon came to signify a set of hanging bells tuned to intervals of the chromatic scale. That meant that there was a bell for each of the notes of the major scale, and all the flats and sharps between them as well. Usually, then, there were 23 bells—two complete chromatic octaves. (In the diatonic, two complete octaves would take 15 bells.)

On a carillon each bell must be in perfect tune. Not only must it be in tune with its sisters, but it must be in tune with itself. A bell when struck does not ring a single tone. It rings at least the first five tones of the harmonic series at one time: an octave below the strike note, the note itself, a minor third above, a perfect fifth, and an octave above. Students of bells (the study is called campanology) give the tones these names: hum tone, strike tone, third, fifth, octave. The very best bells also have two more sounds—an upper third and an upper fifth. New York's Riverside Church has a tenor bell with thirteen recognizable tones.

The word carillon comes from the French word for a four-beat dance.

The bells of the carillon are hung "dead," which means they are stationary. They do not swing back and forth at the tug of a bell rope. Instead, they are struck from inside by a clapper that is worked by a mechanical device. The mechanical device

which operates the carillon is a keyboard (also called a clavier, console, or tablature). It resembles the keyboard of an organ. By means of this keyboard, a single bell ringer or carillonneur makes the clappers strike the bells.

Some carillons are not played by human carillonneurs at all. Instead they are played by a mechanical clockwork device. The tunes in the automatic carillons are set on a revolving drum or barrel and regulated so that tunes will play when the clock mechanism in the bell tower reaches a certain time. The automatic carillon is really a giant music box that plays at the bidding of a time clock. Most musicians agree, though, that the most musical of the carillons are played by human carillonneurs.

When a carillonneur sits down at his keyboard he is alone in a room below the bells or in a room in the very center of the carillon. Often the player strips down to his underwear, for playing is such hard work that it causes the carillonneur to sweat profusely. Playing a carillon is not as simple as playing a piano. The carillonneur must use the sides of his hands on the stiff hand keyboard, his feet on the pedal keyboard. According to one carillonneur, the method of playing is as follows: "The sides of the hands are used, the curved little finger engaging the lever. The stroke is a pressure stroke, the impulse coming from the upper arm muscles. However much it may appear that the performer is 'striking' the lever, very little striking is done . . . the movement is rather a rapid, light pressure than a blow."

Still, though the pressure is light, it must move some very heavy clappers to ring some very heavy bells. The lowest carillon bell is often many tons in weight. The bourdon or tenor bell in Riverside

In 1758, it was written that to play well one needed to be "a musician with a good knowledge of music, good hands and feet, and no gout."

Cathedral in New York weighs 20½ tons and is the biggest tuned bell in the world. Large tuned bells are so expensive that it was once said by an English wit, "Each strike costs a pound."

The very earliest mention of carillons came in the 1400's when a Carmelite prior wrote a history of Egmond Abbey in Holland and reported that its twelfth century abbot had had a "Klokkesel" or bell player made for the gateway. However, it was not for another century that the little striking clocks that rang out the hours automatically, playing tunes on four small bells called "appeelkens," became common. Thus were chimes and then carillons born.

There were primitive chimes, appeelkens, in Middleburg in 1371, Mechlin in 1372, Ghent in 1376, Mons in 1382, and Tournar in 1392. They were the beginnings of the great "singing towers" as carillons are sometimes called.

The number of bells kept growing. So, too, did the numbers of men who could make and play them. In the sixteenth century, carillon fever was running high in Europe. By 1583 the first keyboard had already been invented, for it was mentioned in passing by a visitor to Mechlin.

By the seventeenth century all the principal towns in Europe owned a set of tuned bells.

Early in the seventeenth century two brothers were born who were to become the most famous bellmakers in carillon history. Their names were Frans and Pieter Hemony. During their thirty-two years of bellmaking, the Hemony brothers cast over 50 carillons. They made carillons for Holland, for Belgium's Mechlin and Antwerp Cathedrals, and for cathedrals in Mainz, Hamburg, and else-

Frans was born in 1609, Pieter in 1619.

where. In fact, they were so well known and so well thought of that when Frans moved to Amsterdam in 1654, the town fathers gave him free of charge a building site for his factory.

As soon as a well-tuned carillon was hung in its tower, the search for the carillonneur would begin. Once found, the carillonneur was bound to his job by a contract. A typical contract is this one from July 26, 1681: "I, the undersigned Pieter Châtelet, excellent beiaardier (carillonneur), promise the guild of S. Jacob to play on the beiaard (carillon) on S. Jacob's Day as long as I live, unless I am sick or out of town, for my burial costs." Pieter Châtelet may have signed other contracts with other guilds for his shoes, his house rent, daily meals, and the like.

Carillons continued to be important in Europe through the eighteenth century and well into the nineteenth. At one time there were some forty carillons in Belgium, 60 in the Netherlands, 20 in France and England, and others throughout the rest of Europe. Many of the most beautiful of the European carillons were destroyed in World War I: Ypres, Louvain, Ostend, Roulers, Termonde. They lost their bells in the war and were rebuilt just in time for World War II to devastate Europe again.

In America carillons came late. The first carillon on the North American continent was in Toronto, Canada. The first in the United States was hung in 1922 in the Church of Our Lady of Good Hope in Gloucester, Massachusetts. Today carillons can be heard in Princeton, New Jersey, New York City, Detroit, St. Paul, Philadelphia, and well over 100 other American cities.

Many of the carillons being built today are elec-

New York's Riverside Cathedral has the largest carillon in America. It contains 72 bells of 5 octaves.

tronic. Instead of enormous bells hanging in a gigantic tower, the electronic carillons are small; a carillon of 37 bells "occupies about the space of an upright piano" according to Eric Hatch, an authority on bells. The sound is amplified electronically. There are over 15,000 electronic carillons in the world, and the number is steadily growing.

But whether played electronically, automatically, or by an expert carillonneur who is free of gout, the carillon's distinction lies in its music. It can sing out anything from the most classic piano sonata to national songs, from a light dance tune to a stately church hymn. It is a soothing, beautiful sound, for as the old bell at St. Michael's in Coventry, England, is inscribed: "Music is medicine to the mind."

Chapter 10

Change Ringing

It was a little before eight o'clock in the morning. The churchyard was as silent as the dead who lay within its walls. A slight mist hung over the trees but it was fast disappearing.

Suddenly a distant laugh broke the quiet. It was joined by others. Down the road eight young men were striding, laughing and talking as they came. They were dressed in coats and breeches. Two had caps upon their heads. As they walked, their breaths made little clouds in the air.

One of the youths carried a large leather jug. The others were teasing him about it.

"Give us a pull from the jack," one called out. The jug carrier shook his head, but with a smile.

The eight came into the churchyard. They marched up to the church itself and knocked on the heavy wooden door. The man who opened it gave them a sleepy welcome. They were expected.

The nine men went through the door that led to the belfry but the minister lagged behind.

"Lock it tight, father," the one with the jug

called out as the eight youths climbed the stairs. "Let no one say we escaped afore time."

"Don't worry," came the reply. "I will shut it tight."

And so, on that morning in 1868, the eight members of the Ancient Society of College Youths, an old and revered change ringing society, were locked into the belfry at St. Matthew's church in Bethnal Green in England. They each knew their ropes and their ringing rules. They began ringing at 8:45 in the morning and ended nine hours and twelve minutes later, just before six o'clock. They rang 15,840 changes on the bells without stopping, a record that stood for only four years.

What is change ringing and how did it begin? It is a combination of music, mathematics, and sport. An English pastime, it is also enjoyed by some people in other countries as well.

It is musical because it is played upon bells.

It is mathematical because the ringing of the bells follows precise and intricate mathematical rules.

And it is a sport too, for change ringing is a strenuous, often competitive activity in which intellect and body work together.

But the earliest special ringing on a peal of bells did not engage the mind. Known as "ringing rounds," it was an activity in which the bells were rung one after another, from highest to lowest, over and over and over again. It was a pastime for gentlemen and took a strong back, patience, and a capacity for enjoying boredom.

By the 1600's, when peals of five or more bells hung in many church towers, this kind of bell ring-

Since some men were able to ring 3, 4, or even 5 bells by themselves, the rule in Queen Elizabeth's time was "One man, one bell."

ing was most popular. It was not uncommon for a group of gentlemen to climb to the ringing room of a church tower, one man per each bell rope—with perhaps an extra man to take over from an exhausted friend—and haul upon the ropes for hours on end.

But by the mid-1600's a new and more intricate system of ringing, one that did engage the mind, was growing up. In 1668, Fabian Stedman, who is known as "the father of change ringing," wrote a book on this new system entitled

TINTINNALOGIA
or the

ART OF RINGING
wherein

Is laid down plain and easie Rules for Ringing all sorts of Plain Changes
TOGETHER WITH
Directions for Pricking and Ringing all Cross Peals; with a full Discovery of the Mystery and Grounds of each Peal

AS ALSO

Instructions for Hanging of Bells, with all things belonging thereunto

By a Lover of that ART

Thus change ringing was set down.

Change ringing is a procedure for ringing bells in various orders. Each order is called a change. One of the most important rules in change ringing is that every bell must be played once—but not more than once—in each change.

For example, ringing changes on just three bells means that there are six different ways of ringing those bells. Each method must start with rounds and ends with rounds.

123
213
231
321
312
132
123

There are 120 permutations on five bells. There are 40,320 on eight bells. There are 3,628,800 on ten bells.

Dr. Southey, one of the famous bell specialists, wrote of change ringing: "The very terms are enough to frighten an amateur from any sort of explanation—*hunting, dodging, snapping,* and *place-making; plain bobs, bob-triples, bob-majors;* and even up to *grandsire bob caters*. Heigh-ho! Who can hope to translate all this gibberish to the uninitiated?"

Well, translated it looks something like this: *hunting* is a process of switching places, when a bell moves one place every change and then "hunts its way back to where it began." It rings two consecutive times only—at the front and the back. In the following sequence, the three bell is said to be hunting:

The full changes on twelve bells rung at the rate of one stroke per second would take 137 years.

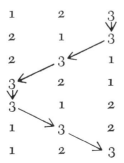

Dodging and place-making are similarly terms for the movement of certain bells in certain changes. The delightful names like majors and caters are the names of peals rung on a particular number of bells: 4-minimus, 5-doubles, 6-minor, 7-triples, 8-major, 9-caters, 10-royal, 11-cinques, 12-maximus. Plain Bob and Grandsire indicate particular methods of ringing, something like a composed piece of music.

The vocabulary is a kind of shorthand or code. And for those who know the secret, it is simple. The names tell what is going to be rung. The first word indicates the method, the second the number of bells on which the changes will be rung. So, a peal of Grandsire Triples means ringing not less than 5,040 changes on seven bells using the Grandsire method.

Change ringing can be a dangerous sport. One expert, Troyte, warned that the coil of rope could get "perhaps round (the learner's) neck, in which case he may be hanged."

An important rule to remember in change ringing is that the rhythm must be regular. The rule applies most rigidly when a group of ringers are ringing a peal. Another rule is that no visual aids to memory are allowed in the bell tower.

Many records have been established in the more than 300 years of change ringing. On Saturday, July 21, 1923, at the Church of St. Chad in Cheshire, England, eight ringers of the Diocesan Guild rang a peal of Kent Treble Bob Major which totaled 17,280 changes and took ten hours to ring. The first complete peal of Grandsire Triples (5,040 changes) was rung in Westminster, England, on Sunday July 7, 1751. Change ringing was done by Paul Revere and his companions in the Old North Church in Boston. But the first peal rung in America was rung in Philadelphia on June 9, 1850, a peal of Grandsire Triples. One of the ringers, a one-legged man, rang steadily for 2¼ hours.

Not everyone, of course, appreciates change ringing. Carillonneurs consider change ringers Philistines who create nothing but noise. According to the musicians, the change ringers—both at practice and in contest—only ring in a cacophony. Indeed, a parish clerk of St. Peter's church in Norfolk, England, who lived near the church in the nineteenth century, was so annoyed by the ringers practicing at 6 on Sunday morning, he penned this verse:

Ye rascally ringers, inveterate foes,
Disturbers of those who are fond of repose,
I wish for the peace and quiet of these lands
That ye had round your necks what ye pull
   with your hands.

Change ringing is still a popular pastime. In fact, new changes are still being composed for bells. One of the latest is called "Wiveliscombe Surprise Major."

One can spend a lovely afternoon listening to the ringing of changes on a peal of bells. It is a pastime that inspires both passionate advocates and passionate protesters. It certainly inspires the ringers. One such, a nineteenth century gentleman named Hezekiah Briggs, who died in 1844, was such a devoted change ringer that he had the following verse carved on his tombstone:

In the United States there are active change-ringing groups in four states and Washington, D.C.

Here lies an old ringer, beneath the cold clay,
Who has rung many peals, both for serious and
   gay,
Through Grandsire and Trebles with ease he
   could range,
Til death called a Bob, which brought round the
   last change.

> "Pull on brave boys, I'm metal to the back,
> But will be hanged before I crack."
> —bell in Towester, England, 1725.

Chapter 11

Bell Ringers

The Scottish night was so dark that not a single star broke through. It was a perfect night for thieves, and they were about their business with swift pleasure.

One thief in particular, a nasty sort named O'Donnell, made his way silently to the local church. It was rumored that the church had a lovely collection of silver altar plates, and it was these that O'Donnell was after.

He had scarcely reached the altar when O'Donnell heard footsteps outside. They seemed to be coming closer. Probably the sexton or the minister on his nightly rounds. But if he saw the door had been broken open . . .

O'Donnell looked about the blackness for a place to hide. In the corner he noticed a long stout rope dangling, but could not make out where it ended.

"I'll just climb up that way," he thought to himself. "High enough to be out of sight should those steps take a turn into the church itself."

But it was O'Donnell's bad luck that the rope

was the bell rope. As he began to climb, the bell set up a clanging that could be heard the town around. It continued even after he dropped down from the rope.

The footsteps rushed into the church, joined by another pair. Both the sexton and the minister were there. They captured O'Donnell with the altar plates stuffed in his trousers. He was sent off to jail for a long time.

As he was led from the church, it is reported that he shouted up to the bell: "If it had not been for thy long tongue and empty head, I would not now be in my present plight."

O'Donnell's problem was not only that he was a thief. It was also that he was not familiar with bells. A bell ringer would not have made such a mistake. Not that bell ringers were considered thieves. Still, they did not always enjoy the best of reputations. Because payment for ringing often was in the form of liquor to fill the ringer's jugs, there was an old saying that

Ringers' jugs, called jacks, were of leather, metal, or earthenware.

> Singers and ringers
> Are little home bringers.

One old bell testifies to this practice of payment. It is inscribed: "Harken do ye heare, our claperes want beere."

The feeling was then, and sometimes is now, that ringing takes little brains and a lot of brawn. Ben Jonson wrote, "If a bell has any sides the clapper will find them."

That bell ringing is a strenuous exercise is true. But there is more to it than simply yanking on a dangling rope. Proper bell ringing takes practice, skill, and experience.

First a bell ringer must understand how a bell is hung. A church bell is hung on a frame on an axle. The bell is rung by pulling on a rope that goes round a wheel that is fastened to the axle. With a ring of bells, the bells are hung like church bells except that, when being rung, their starting position is upside down. In that starting position they have often been described as looking like a nest of baby birds with their mouths open.

It took 50 men pulling on the clapper to ring Tsar Kolokol in Moscow, the biggest bell in the world.

The ringer holds the rope in the crook of his left thumb and the "sallie," the thickened part of the rope, grasped in both hands. Then he pulls. He must pull hard, but not too hard, just hard enough to make the bell lose its balance, swing down, then rise up on the other side and remain upside down again, mouth open. It is not an easy task.

If the ringer pulls too hard, the bell swings around a second time and can pull the ringer up too. Such a mistake is called "overthrowing." There is an old ringer's rhyme from Lincolnshire, England, that goes:

> All ye that do intend to ring
> You undertake a dangerous thing,
> If that a bell you overthrow
> Two pence must pay before you go.

The rules and regulations that were set up differed slightly from one church or ringers' group to another. Often the rules were set down on the wall in humorous verse. From Cornwall in England comes this typical rhyme:

> We ring the quick to church, the dead to grave,
> Good is our use, such usage let us have.
> Who swears, or curses, or in a furious mood
> Quarrels, or strikes, altho he draws no blood,

Who wears a hat, or spurs, or turns a bell,
Or by unskillful handling mars a peall
Let him pay sixpence for each single crime
Twill make him cautious gainst another time.

At first only one man, usually a monk, was assigned to ring a church's bell, and such rules had not been necessary. But once a group of men were in the tower ringing for hours on end, they had to both be compensated for their arduous labor and regulated as any group has to be regulated.

The ringers made up their own rules and abided by them. But for compensation, they banded together into guilds or small unions. The first guild of ringers was formed at Westminster, England. It was recognized by King Henry III in 1254. The Guild's charter reads, in part, "Know all men that we have granted to our Brethern of the Guild of Westminster, who are appointed to ring the great bells there, that they and their successors shall receive annually out of our exchequer 100 shillings."

This was the period of great Guilds in all of Europe.

Ringing Guilds were not very popular, however, even during the period of the crafts guilds. It was not until the seventeenth century that societies of ringers gained importance.

In 1623, Thomas Turner, a merchant of Saffron Walden, was lost in the woods and was guided home by the sound of the town bells. He was so grateful he bequeathed the bell ringers a yearly sum for ringing church bells. So the Saffron Walden Society in Essex, England, began.

Turner also gave money for the yearly preaching of a sermon to the ringers on a day known as "Great Ringing Day."

Ringing clubs were soon started all over England. One of these, the "Ancient Society of College Youths" is still in existence. It was founded on November 5, 1637, and derived its name from the meeting place of its early members—the belfry of St. Martin's College Hall in London. It has counted among its members Fabian Stedman, who is known as "the father of change ringing," and Sir Isaac Newton.

The ringing societies were not trade unions. Rather they were made up of groups of enthusiasts who banded together to help advance the cause of bell ringing and also for the pleasure of ringing bells. Ringing societies went about the English countryside ringing peals in one another's belfries. The societies drew up ringing rules, learned about the care of bells and belfries, and sometimes delved deeply into campanology, the study of bell history.

They also railed against the wearing of hats and spurs while ringing, the hats for politeness' sake, the spurs for the sake of the other ringers. Though there are ringing societies today that ring and study and learn, societies that include women as well as men, spurs at least are no longer a problem.

"Samuel Knight made this ring
In Binstead Steeple for to ding."
—English bell, 1695.

Chapter 12

Bell Houses

The gang of ruffians ran through the streets of the town. Their cries could be heard in the crisp, cold air. Over and over they called:

> The Shalfleet, poor silly people,
> Sold their bells to build a steeple.

But no one paid them any mind. They came every Sunday to shout their nonsense. And nonsense it was. Didn't the bells of Shalfleet ring out to bring in the Lord's Day, and ring out in a steeple as well?

In fact, that same rhyme has been used to taunt town after town throughout the length and breadth of England. And whether it is used against the people of Shalfleet on the Isle of Wight or, in variations, the people of London, Lincolnshire, Staffordshire, and elsewhere, the joke is funnier than it seems at first. No one knows of a town where such a silly thing was ever really done.

But though the joke is one of those nonsense rhymes that begins in obscurity and ends on the city streets where boys and girls jump rope to its rhythms, it proves one thing. People of a parish took their bell houses very seriously.

At first, of course, there was no such thing as a bell house or belfry or bell cote or campanile. The first bells were hung in the churchyard or courtyard where they were to be used. They were hung upon wooden frames or on a bell pole or even upon a tree. What was important was to hang the bell up in a comfortable ringing position, high enough so that the voice of the bell could call out to the farthest village houses and even to the distant farms.

In America, many churches hung ship's bells out in the yard.

After a while, in some countries the simple bell poles were expanded to double poles between which the bell swung. This entire contraption, called a pole belfry, was fastened to the church or meeting house building. Eventually, of course, the pole belfries became a part of the building itself.

In other places, once a parish was firmly established, the parishioners looked around for work to do on their community building. Often they saw that the bell, swinging from its open frame or tree, was being damaged by the winds and rains and, in colder areas, snow. To protect the bell, so much a part of their lives, the parishoners built a frame with a roof, a kind of primitive bell tower.

In Iceland, it is the custom to hang the church bell in the lych gate, a covered entrance to the graveyard.

The next step was a bell cote for one or two bells. Such a cote was attached to the church. In European churches, especially, such bell cotes became dominant features in a church building. They were either open stone cotes or closed wooden ones.

In some churches, the bell cote was never attached to the church building itself but set apart. These detached cotes grew into separate bell towers or campaniles.

However, whether a church is graced with a belfry or a separate campanile, the old saying holds: "Bells were not made for towers, but towers for bells." So it must be understood that bells had a great influence on church architecture from the Middle Ages to our present day.

It is interesting to know that the word belfry is not really related to the word bell. In fact, belfry comes from the Teutonic word *bergfrid*, which meant a movable tower used by besiegers when they tried to climb the great walls surrounding a town. The word then came to mean a tower to protect watchmen, a beacon tower. Finally, the word was used for the tower where the alarum bell was hung and thus for any bell tower.

Just as bells were important to towns early in their history as symbols of freedom, so too the towers became important. As one nineteenth century writer noted: "Every Teutonic burgher community desired to wring the right of erecting such a belfry from its feudal lord."

However important belfries were, it was in Italy that the separate tower, the campanile, reached a peak of architectural perfection. The oldest such towers were built at Ravenna and Classe in the A.D. 500's. They were round like silos. Later ones were usually square, with the famous exception of the Leaning Tower of Pisa. It was begun in 1174 and finished nearly two hundred years later. It leans because the foundation on one side sank and the building had to adjust to the weight of the upper stories so as not to fall.

In Ireland is the oldest existing round bell tower attached to a church.

One of the most beautiful campaniles in the world, some say *the* most beautiful, is the campanile in Florence designed by Giotto. It is 276 feet high and sits on a base that is 45 feet square. It is

richly decorated with the most exquisite marbles, pinks and creams and grays. To come upon it unexpectedly is one of the greatest pleasures a traveler can know.

At first when bell towers and bell houses were built, the architects took great care in placing the bells clear of the walls and making the tower as open as possible. They believed that when the bells were rung, the sound waves would shake the walls and masonry. In fact, one nineteenth century French ringer remarked that the two big bells at Caen made the Norman tower oscillate so badly that he became seasick every time he and his companions rang the bells. However, nowadays sound engineers feel that the best way to hang bells is on an iron frame that is built firmly into the tower walls.

In earlier times the myth about bell ringers going deaf or even dying from an overdose of noise pollution was also common. However, as towers were improved, more and more attention was paid to the lower chamber or solarium where the ringers assembled to pull the ropes of their great bells. Often the room is baffled, sound-proofed, and the ropes snake up through holes in the ceiling. High overhead the bells themselves ring. The sound is so muffled that people standing outside the church can often hear the bells ringing with far more clarity than can the ringers.

A New Haven railroad official fell in love with Italian bell towers and had a campanile built on the Waterbury train station.

Bell towers began simply as a means to protect bells from bad weather. But they became so important in their own right that they influenced the history of architecture. The Florentines think so much of their campanile that they say a pretty girl is *"bello come il campanile*—as pretty as the belfry."

"My sound is good, my shape is neat,
Somebody made me all compleat."
—English bell, Middle Ages.

Chapter 13

Making Bells

The bellmaker glanced nervously at the contract, then at the patient town fathers who waited for him to sign. He read it over again:

And this Witnesseth: That the said master founders engage to found a new carillon of which all the bells shall be altogether and each in itself sonorous, harmonious, melodius, true, solid, good, beautiful, and well finished, and respectively in relation the one to the other, well proportioned, and of a proper and agreeable accord as determined by the best taste and rules of music.

The bellmaker nodded as he read. Surely this was a good contract, for he was a good bellmaker, the best in Belgium he told himself immodestly. He finished reading the contract. It called for the specific number of the bells and the weight of the largest bell was mentioned. All was, in fact, in order.

"I shall be honored to sign," the bellmaker said as he scratched his name onto the parchment with a pen. He added the date, April 1751, with a flourish. "And now gentlemen, I shall work on your bells."

Glass bells were first made as "whimseys" after working hours in English glass factories with left-over glass.

Bells have been made with or without such elaborate contracts for 4,000 years. They have been made of bell metal, silver and gold, wood, pressed glass, porcelain, and earthenware.

Bell making rose to a considerable art in China centuries before it was rediscovered in Europe. The Chinese made huge gongs and great bells of bronze, bells that could comfortably cover a dozen sitting men.

The earliest Christian bells of metal were four-sided iron bells. However, once the bronze casting process was rediscovered in Europe, bigger and better resounding bells were produced.

The process of melting metal, pouring or casting it into a mold and then leaving it to cool and harden is called "founding." Men who design and make bells by this method are called "founders"; the place where they work, a "foundry." The first founders were simply metalworkers who made many different objects besides bells out of metal.

The kind of metal which works best for bells is a mixture of copper and tin, four of five times as much copper as tin. Sometimes minute bits of zinc and lead are added. But silver and gold, despite the poets' "silvery voiced bells," are not used, since bells made of those metals tend to be clanky-sounding and not very resonant. According to founders, the cost of the metal is two thirds of the cost of making the bell.

Just as the first big bells were associated with the churches, so too the first bell founders in Europe were monks. (The earliest instructions on the making of bells are found in a treatise by Walter of Odyngton, an English monk of the thirteenth century.)

Often the bells were cast right in the church courtyard so that they would not have to be transported a long way. Such bells as Great Tom of Lincolnshire and the great bell of Canterbury Cathedral were cast in this fashion. The remains of furnaces in churchyards have been excavated in several places in England and such events were noted occasionally in day books of the period.

The great bell Amphibalus of St. Albans, cast in the 14th century, was cast inside the church in the sacristy hall.

As the art of bellmaking became appreciated, it slowly passed out of the hands of the clergy and into the hands of laymen. In England there were itinerant founders who traveled from churchyard to churchyard casting bells. This remained a custom until as late as the nineteenth century when the railroads made transporting big bells an easier task.

By the fourteenth century, the art of bell casting was well established all over Europe. In fact, by the fifteenth century, competition was so fierce that the English were forbidden by law to import foreign bells.

Today bells are made all over the world. Even in America, the art of bellmaking is a recognized craft. Modern bellmaking is somewhat automated. But though machines take on some of the more arduous tasks, the steps in the crafting of fine bells are essentially the same as they were five centuries ago.

In the 16th century, a tuned bell sold for 30–40 cents a pound. Today the price is $2.00 a pound.

Making a bell requires six main steps: designing the bell, making the patterns or templates, constructing the mold, casting the bell, tuning the bell, and fitting the bell with the clapper. Hanging a

THE PARTS OF A BELL

CROWNSTAPLE
CANONS
CROWN
SHOULDER

WAIST

HIP
SOUND B
LIP
CLAPPE
FLIGHT

big bell is separate from the making, but is an equally important part, for an ill-hung bell is an ill-used bell.

The time it takes to make a large bell varies, but the actual casting of the bell takes only a few minutes. However, the preparation of the designs and templates requires many weeks.

During the design stage, the working drawings are prepared. The bellmaker must understand the vibrations of the particular bell he is designing and how, if he changes the shape of the bell, he changes its tone. The bellmaker must then estimate the weight of the bell metal and order it. All his designs must be made full-size so that they will be accurate. At this stage, the bellmaker is like an architect planning the design of a building.

During the pattern-making stage, the bellmaker constructs the two templates that will be used. They are called "strickle boards." The bellmaker will design one for the outside and one for the inside of the bell.

Constructing the mold, the third step, is a longer task. The molds are metal flasks—usually perforated—that approximate the outer and inner surfaces of the bell. The outer mold is called the bell *case* or *cope*. The inner mold is called the *core*. A special sand or loam is used to make a temporary mold coating.

Meanwhile, the metal—usually a mixture of 80% copper and 20% tin—is being melted in a furnace that is 2,150 degrees F. Then the molten metal is skimmed so that any impurities are removed before the metal is poured. Once the metal is poured slowly and evenly between the molds, it is time to wait. The bell must cool and harden before it is removed. A 500-pound bell can be dug out of the

Inscription from a Gloucestershire bell: "When I was cast into the ground I lost my tone and revived my sound, 1658."

molding pit the very next day. A really large bell might take over a week to cool.

Once cooled and brought out of the pit and unmolded, the bell is usually "aged," or left sitting for a while. Then the bell must be tuned, for no one wants an untuned bell. If the bell is already perfectly in tune and is part of a ring of bells, all of which came out of the pit perfectly in tune, the entire ring is known as a "virgin" or "maiden peal." Such a thing has not happened often.

Usually the bell must be tuned by hand or by machine. The old way of tuning a bell was to chip around the inside or the outside of the part of the bell known as the sound bow with a hammer or chisel. It was a long and hard and very noisy task. Now bells are generally tuned by machine. If the tone of the bell is too low, the tuner must grind off some of the lower edge of the bell. If the tone is too high, the bell must be made thinner with a file.

The early bells were often quite out of tune, for bellmaking was at first not a very exact craft. In fact, at one point an Englishman named Laurence Huddlestone went about the English countryside from church to church with a hammer and a chisel tuning bells that particularly offended his ear.

After a number of years, bell founders discovered that they could regulate the tones of their bells more closely by knowing the exact weight of the metal and the exact measurements of the bell to be cast. In other words, they discovered a precise formula for making the bell "in tune with itself." For of course the bell has more than one note when struck, at least five separate and distinct tones. That is what makes tuning a bell so difficult.

In the nineteenth century a tuning machine was invented. Though the tuning machine is really no

Bell tuners argue about which system for tuning bells is correct: Old Standard or the Simpson principle. They differ by several notes!

more than a vertical lathe, when it was invented bell tuning, too, became scientific.

Once the bell is made and tuned, all that is left is for the clapper and the hanging mechanisms to be installed. However, the bell founder can not yet relax. It is important that the clapper be made as well as the bell. If it is too light, the true deep tones of the bell will never be sounded. If the clapper is too heavy, its every touch will weaken the bell and one day the bell may crack.

Should the bell crack, there are two ways it can be fixed. It may be patched by welding. However, most bellmakers insist that this does not really do the job and the bell will most certainly crack again on the weakened spot. The other, and preferable way, is to break the bell up, melt it down to bell metal once again, and recast it. Many a bell, both new and old, has had this treatment.

Chapter 14

Bellmakers

The monastery was silent. Except for the scraping of sandals along the stone walks, not a sound could be heard. Slowly the monks marched in silent rows to the courtyard where a vast pit had been dug. Then they circled the pit.

At a nod from the choirmaster, and a hummed note from him, seventy-four monks burst into song.

"Hallelujah," they sang. "Praise God in his sanctuary; Praise Him in the firmament of His power; Praise Him for His mighty acts; Praise Him according to His abundant greatness; Praise Him with the blast of the horn; Praise Him with psaltry and harp; Praise Him with timbrel and dance; Praise Him with stringed instruments and the pipe; Praise Him with loud-sounding cymbals; Let everything that hath breath praise the Lord. Hallelujah."

When the last strains of the 150th psalm had trailed off into quiet, the bishop blessed the molten metal that stood steaming in a great vat by the pit.

"Infuse this metal, O Lord," the bishop intoned, "with Your grace and overshadow it with Your power for the honor of Peter, to whom this bell is dedicated and whose name this bell shall bear. In Jesus' name. Amen."

And the circle of monks echoed "Amen."

The abbot nodded a silent command at the four monks standing closest to the vat. They moved noiselessly to their task. The silence then was broken only by the grunting and straining of the monks bending to their work and the hissing of the steaming metal as it cascaded into the pit.

And so the monastery bell was cast.

All bells cast in churches and monasteries had similar rites. Even when bellmaking passed into the hands of the laity, its mysteries were preserved. For example, the famous Bilbie family who were excellent European bellmakers all wore their hair halfway down their backs and consulted strange astrological charts before making or tuning bells.

The first lay bellmakers were also general brass founders. They made pots, mortars, guns, cannon, household items, and artworks besides bells. An early bellmaker was not considered such, he was a *brasiarius*, or brazier. The first brazier to be mentioned specifically as a bellmaker was Fergus of Boston, England, a coppersmith who made two small bells for Croyland Abbey in 1091.

In York Cathedral is a famous 14th century stained glass window dedicated to bell founders and showing many scenes in the bellmaking process.

Since European craftsmen and laborers often took their surnames from their businesses, the sign of how popular a craft was is how often the name has come down through the centuries. In England, for example, there are still many Bellfounders, Bellgetters, Bellmans, and Bells.

The first Englishman to have regularly followed the profession of bell founding was Roger de Ropeforde who, in 1284, cast four bells for Exeter Cathedral.

Bell founding lost some popularity after the Reformation, for bells seemed to many just another instance of the "popish practices." However, it was revived again in Queen Elizabeth's time. In fact, the English "golden age of bell founding" was from 1630–1750. In the rest of Europe, bell founding reached its peak with the Hemony brothers in the early 1600's, who cast so many lovely carillons.

In America, the most famous bellmaker was Paul Revere. Thirty-seven of the forty-eight big bells he cast are still in existence.

Paul Revere became a bell founder by accident. He was a silversmith by trade. But when the bell in Boston's Old North Church cracked in 1792, he was asked to fix it. He rode to Abington to talk to a foundryman, Aaron Hobart, and came back with Hobart's foreman. The bell they cast was, to the ears of many, "harsh and shrill." But Revere was a man who could learn from experience, and he was a superb craftsman. He realized how little he knew of bell casting and began to study it. Today his bells are known for their excellent tone. Revere himself noted this on the inscription of his masterpiece, the King's Chapel bell in Boston which he cast the year before he died. "The sweetest bell we ever made. Paul Revere & Son, 1817" reads the inscription.

The first woman founder was an American, Mrs. A. S. C. Forbes, who founded in California in the 1900's.

Such an inscription was not unusual on bells. Indeed early founders, like artists, signed their works either with their names and dates or with a symbol. The inscriptions were put on the mold before the bell was cast.

As bellmaking progressed, the inscriptions became more elaborate, sometimes in rhyme. For ex-

ample, from Himbleton, England, comes this inscription on one of a peal of bells:

> John Martin of Worcester he made wee
> Be it known to all that do wee see, 1675.

The earliest bells had Roman or Saxon lettering
and Latin inscriptions because, of course, they
were made by monks. Often between each word
in the inscription would be a cross. In the fourteenth century, Gothic lettering came into fashion.
And by the seventeenth century, Roman capital
letters were the rule.

On many of the earliest bells the inscriptions
were merely the names of the saints to whom the
bells were dedicated. Sometimes, though, passages
from scripture, or memorials to the donors were
added. This from Lincolnshire in England is typical:

> I. H. C. CAMPANA BEATE MARIE
> IOHANNES POTTER ME FACIT

> Jesus, the bell of the blessed Mary,
> John Potter made me.

By the seventeenth century, the inscriptions
were colloquial, sometimes humorous, boasting, or
even silly:

> All you of Bathe that heare mee sound
> Thank Lady Hopton's hundred pound.

>   and

> Mankind like me are often found
> Possessed of nought but empty sound.

Occasional bells boasted of a founder's prowess,
or even twitted a rival:

> Bilby and Bosh may come and see
> What Evans and Nott have done by me, 1758.

And quite a number of bells were inscribed to commemorate historical events, such as:

> But I, for pride, the greater Marlborough bear;
> Terror of tyrants and the soul of war.

or

> The King, Pitt, and Quebec for ever, 1760.

Not all inscriptions are of the highest literary merit, but when they rise to heights they speak about the history and lure of bells from their beginnings.

This poem, inscribed line by line on each of a ring of eight bells in Cornwall, somehow seems to sum up 4,000 years of bell history:

Treble: By music minds an equal temper know
    2: Nor swell too high nor sink too low
    3: Music the fiercest grief can charm
    4: And fate's severest rage disarm
    5: Music can soften pain to ease
    6: And make despair and madness please
    7: Our joys below it can improve
Tenor: And antidate the bliss above.

—St. Austel, 1810.

"If you have a judicious ear
You'll own my voice is sweet and clear."
—bell in London, 1777.

Chapter 15

Bells in Poetry and Song

Listen again to the names of some bells. The list
is like a song. It is like a prayer. It is like a mighty
spell:

> Oven bell,
> Vesper bell,
> Passing bell,
> Soul,
> Labour bell,
> Advent bell,
> Sanctus bell,
> School.
> Catch-cope and Judas bells,
> Compline and
> Storm,
> Tocsin bell,
> Sermon bell,
> Pudding, and
> Doom.

Those are just a few of the many bells that have
rung throughout history. And the history of bells
is full of beauty, poetry, and song.

Bells and music—it is a natural association, for

bells can play tunes. But bells and poetry? If you look again carefully, you will see that the story of bells is full of rhythm and rhyme.

Many of the inscriptions on medieval bells ring with rhythmic life:

> My sound is good, my shape is neat,
> Somebody made me all compleat.

and

> I sweetly tolling men do call
> To taste on meats that feed the soul.

The names of individual bells throb with the life of poetry: Tsar Kolokol, Great Tom, Big Ben. Say the names of the seven bells of old Croyland Abbey and you will see they make a poem:

> Pega,
> Bega,
> Tatwin, Tusketyl,
> Betelin, Bartholomew, and
> Guthlac.

And many of the most famous poets the world has ever known have sung of bells, right up to the present day.

HOW SOFT THE MUSIC
OF THOSE VILLAGE BELLS
by William Cowper

Cowper, an English poet who lived from 1731–1800, is best known for his comic "John Gilpin's Ride."

How soft the music of those village bells
Falling at intervals upon the ear
In cadence sweet, now dying all away,
Now pealing loud again, and louder still,
Clear, sonorous, as the gale comes on!
With easy force it opens all the cells
Where memory slept. Wherever I have heard
A kindred melody, the scene recurs,

And with it all its pleasures and its pains.
Such comprehensive views the spirit takes,
That in a few short moments I retrace
(As in a map the voyager his course)
The windings of my way through many years.

THOSE EVENING BELLS
by Thomas Moore

Those evening bells! those evening bells!
How many a tale their music tells
Of youth, and home, and that sweet time
When last I heard their soothing chime!

Those joyous hours are passed away;
And many a heart that then was gay,
Within the tomb now darkly dwells,
And hears no more those evening bells.

And so 'twill be when I am gone,—
That tuneful peal will still ring on;
While other bards shall walk these dells,
And sing your praise, sweet evening bells.

An Irish poet of the early nineteenth century, Moore was the author of some of the most beloved songs in the English language. "Believe Me If All Those Endearing Young Charms" is one of them.

GAY GO UP
Anon

Gay go up and gay go down,
To ring the bells of London town.

Halfpence and farthings
Say the bells of St. Martin's.

Oranges and lemons,
Say the bells of St. Clemon's.

Pancakes and fritters,
Say the bells of St. Peter's.

Two sticks and an apple,
Say the bells of Whitechapel.

This old English nursery rhyme names most of the best-known churches in London.

Kettles and pans,
Say the bells of St. Anne's.

You owe me ten shillings,
Say the bells of St. Helen's.

When will you pay me?
Say the bells of Old Bailey.

When I grow rich,
Say the bells of Shoreditch.

Pray when will that be?
Say the bells of Stepney.

I am sure I don't know,
Says the great bell of Bow.

THE BELLS
Edgar Allan Poe
(Inspired by the sound of church bells
reaching him through his open window)

I

Hear the sledges with the bells,
        Silver bells!
What a world of merriment their melody foretells!
    How they tinkle, tinkle, tinkle,
        In the icy air of night!
    While the stars, that oversprinkle
    All the heavens, seem to twinkle
        With a crystalline delight;
        Keeping time, time, time;
        In a sort of Runic rime,
To the tintinnabulation that so musically wells
    From the bells, bells, bells, bells,
            Bells, bells, bells—
    From the jingling and the tinkling of the bells.

II

Hear the mellow wedding bells,
        Golden bells!

Poe, who lived from 1809–1849, was one of America's greatest story writers. He is considered the father of modern mystery and detective tales. His most famous poem is called "The Raven."

What a world of happiness their harmony foretells!
  Through the balmy air of night
  How they ring out their delight!
    From the molten-golden notes,
      And all in tune.
    What a liquid ditty floats
To the turtle-dove that listens, while she gloats
      On the moon!
  Oh, from out the sounding cells,
What a gush of euphony voluminously wells!
      How it swells!
      How it dwells
    On the future! how it tells
    Of the rapture that impels
  To the swinging and the ringing
    Of the bells, bells, bells,
  Of the bells, bells, bells, bells,
      Bells, bells, bells—
To the riming and the chiming of the bells!

III

  Hear the loud alarum bells,
      Brazen bells!
What a tale of terror, now, their turbulency tells!
  In the startled ear of night
  How they scream out their affright!
    Too much horrified to speak,
    They can only shriek, shriek,
      Out of tune,
In a clamorous appealing to the mercy of the fire,
In a mad expostulation with the deaf and frantic fire,
    Leaping higher, higher, higher,
    With a desperate desire,
   And a resolute endeavor
   Now—now to sit or never,
  By the side of the pale-faced moon.
    Oh, the bells, bells, bells!
    What a tale their terror tells
      Of Despair!

How they clang, and clash, and roar!
What a horror they outpour
On the bosom of the palpitating air!
Yet the ear it fully knows,
By the twanging,
And the clanging,
How the danger ebbs and flows;
Yet the ear distinctly tells,
In the jangling
And the wrangling
How the danger sinks and swells—
By the sinking or the swelling in the anger of the bells,
Of the bells—
Of the bells, bells, bells, bells,
Bells, bells, bells—
In the clamor and the clangor of the bells!

IV

Hear the tolling of the bells,
Iron bells!
What a world of solemn thought their monody com-
pels!
In the silence of the night
How we shiver with affright
At the melancholy menace of their tone!
For every sound that floats
From the rust within their throats
Is a groan.
And the people—ah, the people,
They that dwell up in the steeple,
All alone,
And who tolling, tolling, tolling
In that muffled monotone,
Feel a glory in so rolling
On the human heart a stone—
They are neither man nor woman,
They are neither brute nor human,
They are ghouls;
And their king it is who tolls;

And he rolls, rolls, rolls,
    Rolls
  A paean from the bells,
  And his merry bosom swells
  With the paean of the bells;
And he dances, and he yells;
    Keeping time, time, time,
    In a sort of Runic rime,
To the paean of the bells,
    Of the bells:
    Keeping time, time, time,
    In a sort of Runic rime,
  To the throbbing of the bells,
Of the bells, bells, bells—
    To the sobbing of the bells;
  Keeping time, time, time,
    As he knells, knells, knells,
  In a happy Runic rime,
    To the rolling of the bells,
    Of the bells, bells, bells:
    To the tolling of the bells,
  Of the bells, bells, bells, bells,
    Bells, bells, bells—
To the moaning and the groaning of the bells.

EIGHT BELLS
American Sea Chanty

My husband's a saucy foretopman,
A chum of the cook's, don't you know.
He put his head down the cook's funnel
And shouted, "Come up from below!"

    Eight bells! Eight bells!
    Rouse out there the watch from below!
    Eight bells! Eight bells!
    Rouse out there the watch from below!

My matey once shipped on a whaler
That sailed to the far northern seas,

This is an American sea chanty, sung with gusto by the sailors as they worked. Chanties helped the men pass the time and kept them all moving in the same rhythm at their tasks. The eight bells marked the changing of the watch at sea.

And being a bold-hearted sailor,
He cared not for ice, sea, nor breeze.

> Eight bells! Eight bells!
> Rouse out there the watch from below!
> Eight bells! Eight bells!
> Rouse out there the watch from below!

At the end of his watch, though, his fancy
Was to get to his bunk quickly, O,
For he wanted to dream of his Nancy,
So he called to the watch, "Hi, below!"

> Eight bells! Eight bells!
> Rouse out there the watch from below!
> Eight bells! Eight bells!
> Rouse out there the watch from below!

POEM
by Emily Dickinson

Emily Dickinson was a recluse in 19th century New England who wrote nearly 2,000 poems, some of them the loveliest in the English language.

How still the Bells in Steeples stand
Till swollen with the Sky
They leap upon their silver Feet
In frantic Melody!

I HEARD THE BELLS ON CHRISTMAS DAY
by Henry Wadsworth Longfellow

Longfellow was probably the most famous and popular American poet of the 1800's. Among his poems are "Paul Revere's Ride" and "The Village Blacksmith."

I heard the bells on Christmas day
Their old, familiar carols play,
And wild and sweet the words repeat
    Of peace on earth, good-will to men.

I thought how, as the day had come,
The belfries of all Christendom
Had rolled along the unbroken song
    Of peace on earth, good-will to men.

And in despair I bowed my head:
"There is no peace on earth," I said,

"For hate is strong and mocks the song,
  Of peace on earth, good-will to men."

Then pealed the bells more loud and deep:
"God is not dead, nor doth he sleep;
The wrong shall fail, the right prevail,
  With peace on earth, good-will to men."

Till, ringing, singing on its way,
The world revolved from night to day,
A voice, a chime, a chant sublime,
  Of peace on earth, good-will to men!

POEM
by e. e. cummings

(b
    eLl
        s?
            bE

-ginningly)come-swarm:faces
ar;rive go.faces a(live)
sob bel
ls

(pour wo
          (things)
                    men
                        selves-them

inghurl)bangbells(yawnchurches
suck people)reel(dark-
ly)whirling
in

(b
    ellSB
        el
            Ls)

*Edward Estlin Cummings, a
modern lyric poet, is best
known for his disregard of
the rules of punctuation. But
underneath the spelling and
punctuation tricks is a joyous, simple hymn to bells.*

-to sun(crash). Streets
glit
ter
a,strut:do;colours;are:m,ove

o im
     -pos-
          sibl
               y

(ShoutflowereD
flowerish boom
b el Lsb El l
s!cry)

(be
    llsbe
         lls)
              b
               (be
                   llsbell)
                          ells
                             (sbells)

The poets have said it: bells shout, cry, bang,
according to e. e. cummings; they peal, ring, sing,
according to Longfellow; they toll, chime, clang,
according to Poe. They do all this and have done
all this for over four thousand years. Bells, it seems,
have touched all forms of human endeavor. They
continue to touch us today.

There is a bell in Northamptonshire, England,
that seems most suitably inscribed. It says simply,
touchingly, yet so truly, what bells have done for
so many centuries:

I MEASURE LIFE: I BEWAIL DEATH.

Bibliography

Anthony, Dorothy Malone, *The World of Bells*. Des Moines, Iowa: Wallace-Homestead Book Co., 1971.

Botkin, B. A., and Harlow, Alvin F., *A Treasury of Railroad Folklore*. New York: Crown Publishers, 1953.

Coffin, Tristam P., *The Book of Christmas Folklore*. New York: The Seabury Press, 1973.

Coleman, Satis, *Bells, Their History, Legends, Making, and Uses*. Chicago: Rand McNally, 1928.

────── *The Book of Bells*. New York: The John Day Co., 1938.

Davis, William Stearnes, *Life on a Mediaeval Barony*. New York: Harper, 1923, 1951.

Fielding, "The Occult Lore of Bells" from *The Second Occult Review Reader,* edited by B. J. Hurwood. New York: Award Books, 1969.

Gatty, Rev. Alfred, *The Bell Its Origin, History, and Uses*. London: George Ball, 1848.

Hatch, Eric, *The Little Book of Bells*. New York: Duell, Sloan, & Pearce, 1964.

MacGregor, Alasdair Alpin, *The Peat-Fire Flame*. Edinburgh & London: The Ettrick Press, 1937.

Maple, Eric, "Bells" from *Man, Myth, & Magic* #8, 1970.

Meneely Bell Co., Troy, New York, pamphlet 1912.

Morris, Ernst, *Legends o' the Bells*. London: Sampson Low, Marston & Co., Ltd., 1938.

Morrison, Gouverneur, *Bells, Their History and Romance*. Santa Barbara: J. F. Rowny Press, 1932.

New England Magazine, January, 1891, pp. 547–569.

Nichols, J. R., *Bells Thro' the Ages.* London: Chapman & Hall Ltd., 1928.

Puckle, Bertram S., *Funeral Customs: Their Origins and Development.* New York: Frederick A. Stokes Co., 1926.

Raven, J. J., *The Bells of England.* London: Methuen & Co., 1906.

Rice, William Gorham, *Carillon Music and Singing Towers of the Old World and the New.* New York: Dodd, Mead & Co., 1925.

Sayers, Dorothy L., *The Nine Tailors.* New York: Harcourt, Brace & World, 1934.

Sloane, Eric, *The Sound of Bells.* New York: Doubleday & Co., 1966.

Springer, L. Elisonore, *The Collector's Book of Bells.* New York: Crown Publishers, Inc., 1972.

Stahlschmidt, J. C. L., *Surrey Bells and London Bell Founders.* London: Elliot Stock, 1884.

Strutt, Joseph, *The Sports and Pastimes of the People of England.* London: Chatto & Windus, 1876.

Tyack, Rev. Geo. S., *A Book About Bells.* London: William Andrews & Co., 1898.

Walsh, Marie T., *The Mission Bells of California.* San Francisco: Harr Wagner Publishing Co., 1934.

Walters, H. B., *Church Bells of England.* Oxford: Oxford University Press, 1912.

Index